His Name Is Today

His Name Is Today

Bob Macauley and AmeriCares

Bill Halamandaris

Jameson Books
Ottawa, Illinois

Titles from Jameson Books are available at special discounts for bulk purchases, for sales promotions, premiums, fund raising or educational use. Special condensed or excerpted paperback editions can also be created to customer specifications.

For information and other requests please write
Jameson Books, Inc., 722 Columbus Street,
P.O. Box 738, Ottawa, Illinois 61350

Mail Orders: 800-426-1357
Telephone: 815-434-7905
Facsimile: 815-434-7907
Email: jamesonbooks@yahoo.com

Printed in the United States of America.

Jameson Books are distributed to the book trade by MidPoint Trade Books, 27 West 20th Street, Suite 1102, New York, NY 10011. Bookstores please call 212-727-0190 to place orders.

Bookstore returns should be addressed to MidPoint Trade Books, 1263 Southwest Boulevard, Kansas City, KS 66103.

ISBN: 0-915463-93-8

6 5 4 3 2 1 09 08 07 06 05

His Name Is Today

We are guilty of many errors and many faults,
but our worst crime is
abandoning the children,
neglecting the fountain of life.
Many of the things we need can wait.
The child cannot.

Right now is the time
his bones are being formed,
his blood is being made
and his senses are being developed.

To him we cannot answer "Tomorrow."
His name is "Today."

GABRIELA MISTRAL OF CHILE

For Leila with love

Contents

Forewords

I can't say enough good things about Bob Macauley. He is a great personal friend of all the Bushes, and he is an example to us all.

Bob has learned the secret of life, and he has shared that secret with the rest of us. He knew when he had enough, so he started helping others who did not. He knew that all of us wanted to help but didn't know how, so he showed us. Bob taught us all that by giving we receive.

Bob cuts red tape and when he sees a need, he takes care of the problem, whether here or abroad. He lets nothing stand in the way of helping people in any way he can.

I could not have asked for a better friend than Bob. He is an inspiration to me.

Barbara Bush

It is hard for me to be objective about Bob Macauley. He has been a close friend for many years. I love the guy. I admire him. It is just that simple.

Bob became a friend way back in grade school. We kept up our friendship through boarding school, and through the years that led to my presidency.

Bob was a bit of a renegade. He marched, at times, to a different drummer. He was and remains a free spirit. A man of means, he never lacked the common touch, never lacked concern for others.

Bob Macauley is truly what I refer to as a Point of Light. AmeriCares bears his personal commitment to helping others, both here and abroad. He *is* AmeriCares; and what a job he has done.

I repeat: The thing that makes Bob so special is that he feels so deeply about helping others. It is not just doing a job or fulfilling a responsibility. For him, helping those in need comes right from his caring heart.

I admire him. He has set the bar very high for other organizations dedicated to helping others.

AmeriCares has kept the overhead down, the service to others up.

Bob has been very sick. I just hope that God continues to give him the strength he needs to carry on in his life of service.

George H. W. Bush

The Pope and the President

*I*n October 2000, my wife Angela and I are invited to attend a benefit for the international relief organization AmeriCares. Long the largest private relief agency in the world, AmeriCares has just passed a major milestone: the delivery of two billion dollars in life-saving medicines and medical supplies to 110 countries around the globe.

We are seated at the head table along with the guests of honor, George and Barbara Bush. Through no merit of my own, I have been given the honor of sitting next to the former First Lady. Inevitably and almost immediately the conversation turns to our mutual friends, the Macauleys, and what they have done with AmeriCares.

After a few minutes, Mrs. Bush looks directly at me and says, "You know, someone really should tell Bob's story." It is a question more than a statement. I said I wasn't sure he would allow it and left her question hanging in midair.

When it is time for his keynote address, former President Bush stands and takes the stage. "You know, I have been very fortunate," he says. "I have had a chance to meet most of the world's leaders. I have met presidents, prime ministers, religious leaders and a lot of remarkable men and women. I don't impress easily. But I have to say I am in awe of Bob Macauley and what he has done with AmeriCares."

On September 13, 1981, Bob Macauley is given a private audience with Pope John Paul II. Bob, who is not Catholic, is there as Chairman of the Board of Covenant House, a shelter for runaway kids founded by Father Bruce Ritter. Ritter and Macauley discuss this organization's efforts to aid children of the night with the Pope and present him with a scrapbook prepared by Covenant House.

The Pope examines the scrapbook page by page and focuses on the image of a twelve-year-old girl named Gloria.

She is slight and fair with haunting dark eyes.

"What is her story?" the Pope asks. Macauley explains she is a runaway who had been working the streets when they found her. Not knowing the Italian word for prostitute, he says she has been working as a "hooker."

Unfamiliar with the slang expression, the Pope is puzzled. When the meaning of the word is explained to him, he returns to the photograph and gazes intently at it until tears form in his eyes. Slowly, almost reluctantly, he turns the page.

The dialogue then turns to Poland. The Pope says his people there are suffering under martial law, many dying for lack of medicines readily available elsewhere. Noting Bob's extraordinary success fund raising for Covenant House, the Pope asks if he will try to do something to help the people of Poland.

"Certainly, Your Holiness," Bob responds.

Later, remembering this fateful moment, Bob laughs. "What else could I say? 'No, Pope?'" The thought is inconceivable. Before Macauley leaves, he has promised he will raise $50,000 to help buy medicine for the Polish people.

Who is this man a President of the United States finds awesome and the Pope asks for favors? What makes him so special? What are the lessons of his remarkable life?

"To reach the port of Heaven,

We must sail sometimes with the wind,

And sometimes against it.

But we must sail, and not drift, or lie at anchor."

ROBERT C. MACAULEY

The One and Only

*I*t is June of 1989. I have traveled from Washington, D.C., to Connecticut with a camera crew to meet Bob Macauley. It is four years since I tired of turning over rocks for the U. S. Senate, eighteen years after that effort began.

Congressional oversight is a sad and cynical process. I was good at it and took some initial delight in chasing bad guys, trying to protect the taxpayer and keep the vultures from drinking too deeply at the public trough. But the cumulative weight of this battle has taken its toll on me, and the Senate has begun to change. Increasingly, those drawn to political process are becoming polemical. The new breed seems more self-serving than public servants, more interested in taking than giving.

As an antidote to my own growing depression, I "do a 180" in 1985 and decide to begin looking for people who represent the best of our society instead of the worst, for what works as opposed to what does not. While I begin this quest proclaiming noble motives and high objectives, in truth, it is a highly personal odyssey. I am looking for hope. I am looking for a way to get to know and learn from the best people I can find. I am looking for an antidote to the evening news.

When I ask him whom he most admires, Peter Grace tells me about Bob Macauley. The words he uses to describe Macauley are effusive. "He is the most talented, artistic, energized, and charitably-motivated individual I have ever met," Grace says. "He's so good he is almost unbelievable. He truly believes nothing is impossible."

After a year of investigation, I am inclined to believe Grace is right. Like President Bush, but with far less cause, I am already in awe of Bob Macauley.

This is before Macauley sent a helicopter into a war zone to rescue one child, before he rebuilt

African-American churches fire-bombed in the south, before the Sudan and Rwanda, before Armenia and Chernobyl, before the free clinics and the camp he started for terminally-ill kids.

Still, how could you *not* be in awe of a man who would mortgage his own home to save a couple of hundred orphans from another land, put planes in the air on a mercy flight to what was then Soviet territory before he had permits to land, send to children abroad tankers of chocolate for Christmas, and leverage his personal connections not only to make good the marker he had given the Pope in 1982 but to exceed that goal by millions?

I am anxious to meet the man who practices such fearless philanthropy, the man Grace described as "the one and only." I find him on the top floor of a modest office building in New Canaan. The hallways leading to Macauley's office invite a review of the many medals, citations, and commendations AmeriCares has received from the presidents of various countries in South America, Africa, and Asia. There are also framed letters of support from presidents Nixon, Ford, Carter, and Reagan.

In contrast to the nondescript and rather drab nature of the rest of the building, Bob's office is painted a peaceful forest green. There is a massive desk facing an oversized leather couch. Pastoral paintings, candid photos of his wife and two children, and a number of images of the Pope and Mother Teresa decorate the walls. The 1984 President's Voluntary Action Award hangs near the door.

I look around the room and make notes while the camera crew sets up for the interview. The letters from Mother Teresa compel attention. "God loves you for all the love you share with God's poor through your gifts," one of Mother's letters reads. Another expresses thanks: "My gratitude is my prayer for you that you may grow more and more in the likeness of Christ through love and compassion." "Please pray for me," a third letter asks, "as I do for you."

When Bob comes in he fills the room. You are immediately conscious of the sheer size of the man—6'3" and 230 pounds—but it is more than that. There is the big "hello," the deep, booming voice, the hearty handshake, and the gracious manner of a natural-born salesman, but it is more than that as well.

A relentless sense of energy arrives with him. While he is nothing but courteous and solicitous, everything suddenly seems to move at a faster pace. On a level hard to describe comes the awareness that one is in rare company.

I am conscious I am dealing with a busy man who has a multi-million dollar business to run as well as an international foundation; so after a brief exchange of pleasantries, I ask him to take a seat and promise to keep our intrusion to a minimum. Dutifully, he takes a position on the sofa and puts me at ease. Seemingly, he has all the time in the world. The camera crew makes last minute adjustments, turns on the lights, and signals that they are ready.

"Let's begin," I tell Bob. And the cameras roll.

I explain what we are doing and why, and start the interview. I ask four questions and find we have already talked for an hour and a half. Somehow Bob anticipates and answers all the other questions I came prepared to ask but never got around to, so when he asks if I have all the tape I need, I say "yes" even though I am reluctant to have our conversation end. To my surprise, he asks me to dismiss the crew and

11

stay a while longer if I can. We close the door and talk for two more hours.

We part as friends, already talking about the next time we can get together. Somehow a bond has been created where there seems to be no reason for one. I have no idea why he seems to have taken an interest in me, but on my end the connection is clear. I have found the role model I have been looking for. A line comes to me from somewhere as I leave: "He is what every man hopes to be when young and wishes he were when he has grown old."

It is the spring of 2002. My wife Angie and I are visiting with the Macauleys at their home in Palm Beach. It is something we have done on a recurring basis through the years. At first, I would travel alone to visit with Bob and Leila in Connecticut three or four times a year. Bob and I would spend long hours in his study in New Canaan talking about life, love and marriage, fishing, poetry, and music. We'd talk about everything and nothing, but most of all we'd talk about what was going on in the world and what we could do to make things better.

When I visit, the television is always on with the sound off. Bob has the remote in his hand as we talk and surfs the channels, looking for someone to help. As someone later said, he is the kind of man who reads the New York Times *with a telephone in his hand. Proof of that is that there are three phone and two fax lines coming into the house. When you visit the Macauleys, you quickly get used to hearing them go off at all hours of the night. Often in the middle of the night, you hear a deep voice that could only be Bob's answer, and you wonder when—if ever—he sleeps.*

He seems at this time to sit astride the universe. He knows everyone and has an intimate understanding of everything going on in every corner of the globe. He is a great story-teller and fascinating company. The first question he asks when I arrive is always, "Have you heard about what's going on in . . ." some distant place he names, followed by a lengthy dialogue about the problem.

Almost naturally when I marry, "I" becomes "we."

"I have an excellent grapevine as you know," Bob wrote in 1993. "I hope you heard the shriek of Eureka! when I learned that you were about to be affianced."

The letter expresses his delight at my good fortune and reminds me we had an agreement that he would meet the young lady I would marry before we wed to "corroborate" my feelings. At a meeting arranged for that purpose a month later, both Leila and Bob are quick to embrace the woman who is to be my wife, so much so that thereafter Bob always reminds me that I am not allowed to visit without her. With that, Angie and I begin our yearly migrations north and south with the seasons to visit the Macauleys.

Though it has only been a few months since we saw them last in New York, it is clear Bob is not doing well. The weather in Florida has been bad, making it difficult to get outside where the sun can bake the ache out of his bones. Worse, he hasn't been able to get into the pool for hydrotherapy—the only form of exercise his battered body can now tolerate.

The arthritis he has had since I have known him has now spread to his jaw, making it difficult at times for him to talk. Now that he is unable to venture out, his world seems reduced to the size of his living room where he spends most of the day, sitting in an overstuffed armchair. His breath is labored. Walking is difficult. Increasingly, even the smallest tasks prove troublesome and vexing.

Though nothing is said, we can feel Bob's pain and see the fear in Leila's eyes as we leave. In the next few weeks

Bob's condition continues to deteriorate. When it is finally warm enough to return home, he has to be transported by medivac.

Long ago I determined one of my goals would be to live a life of limited regrets. Bob's declining health stays on my mind and forces an issue that has long lain dormant. I knew Bob's story needed to be told. And I knew that if I didn't at least offer to try to tell it, I would always regret it.

By summer Bob's health has stabilized. The weather up north has been more agreeable. Leila has found some medical assistance, arranged for live-in help and therapy. Bob is beginning to exercise again. When we speak on the phone, he sounds like his old self. It is hard to imagine there is anything wrong with him.

But the truth is evident in the fact that for the first time he is unable to attend an AmeriCares gala. Leila says he simply isn't up to it. This confirms my sense that it is time to tell him what is on my mind. When we return home from the gala, I decide to send him a letter.

"You know, I have always believed in teaching by example," I write. "I don't know of a better example of the way we all should aspire to live our lives than the two of you."

I go on to tell him I have chosen the formal communication of a letter because I want to lay out the parameters of the project as I see it—the purpose, the process, and the benefit. I say that I will cover my own expenses and donate any royalties I might receive to charity.

"My goal would be to write a book that would touch as many people as possible," I conclude, "and benefit AmeriCares in the process."

I know a number of others have made similar requests. We have talked about several offers for book projects and movie deals through the years. I also know how little Bob likes personal publicity. "I detest ego," he has said to me more times than I can remember. "To me it is just another form of selfishness."

And so I fully expect he will decline my offer. To my surprise, he says, "Yes."

Over the course of the year that follows, we step up our visits. They are like many conversations we have had before, but now I come armed with questions and a tape recorder.

During the first of these visits in the fall, we discuss the elements of the project and develop a lengthy list of people who should be interviewed. With the help of Annie Weirether, Bob's right hand at Ameri-Cares, I contact everyone on the list and explain what I have in mind. Almost to a man, they welcome the project and express a desire to participate.

I begin interviewing people in January of 2003 and quickly get in the habit of calling Bob after each interview to bounce what has been said against his extraordinary memory. Increasingly, as we work together, I realize I have been uniquely prepared for this project. I soon develop the firm impression that this book is more his idea than mine.

Halfway through the project, I mention this radical thought to Annie. She surprises me by not being surprised. She laughs and says, "That would be just like him."

Seeds of Giving

ob remembers a boy who came up from the South when he was in the sixth grade at Greenwich Country Day School. "He was kind of an odd kid," Bob said, *"and didn't quite fit in. We had a very tightly knit clique. He looked different and talked different."*

Most of the other kids made fun of the Southern boy and gave him a hard time, but Bob befriended him. "He was a long way from home," Bob says. "I used to invite him over to our place on Saturdays and weekends to play." The boy's mother was so grateful she sought out Bob's mother at graduation and thanked her for Bob's kindness. Bob never thought much about it.

In 1982, Bob is trying to figure out how to keep his promise to the Pope and looking for whatever assistance he can find. He has had volunteers call the leading pharmaceutical companies begging for help. One of the volunteers opens a door at the Richardson Vicks Corporation and sets up an appointment. Two days later, Bob and his associate travel to the company's headquarters in Wilton to meet with the community affairs director.

The community affairs director listens politely as Bob tells his story, but is noncommittal. As they are about to leave, Bob asks if he can stop by the chairman's office to pay his respects. The director of community affairs is not optimistic but says he will see if it is possible. He has been with the company for several years and rarely had a private audience with Mr. Richardson himself. To his surprise, the chairman readily agrees.

When they enter the office, Bob's childhood friend, now Chairman of the Richardson Vicks Corporation, greets him warmly. After they have embraced, Richardson turns to his employee and asks why they are there.

"We are trying to see if we can get some vitamins and medicines for Mr. Macauley's foundation," the man explains.

"Not if," the Chairman responds. "When."

By the time Bob returns home, the office has already received word there is a freight car full of over-the-counter medications and vitamins on the way from a Richardson Vicks subsidiary in California. The gifts, millions of pounds of patent medicines, continue for years.

"Funny how things always come back," Bob says.

It is the fall of 2002. I sit, as is my custom when visiting Bob, on the floor facing him with my back against the sofa in their living room. Bob is seated in his leather chair near the stone fireplace. The tape recorder and a stack of tapes are on the floor between us.

We are in his home in upstate New York. Bob has always liked the serenity of a rural life. This home is the third incarnation of his version of a family farm. It is lovely though modest for a man of his means. There are bedrooms for each of their two children,

Melinda and Robert, now grown, and a guest room, but no superfluous space. There are no hordes of servants, butlers, and maids.

The most striking feature of the house is the walls, which look like cypress paneling but are actually composed of cypress trees Bob has had hauled up from the bottom of a swamp in Alabama. They have been cut to form eighteen square inch logs and formed into a modern variation of the classic log cabin. The walls are decorated with family photos, religious artifacts, sketches and drawings by Bob's sister, Sheila. Bob's chair faces plate glass windows overlooking a small lake set in the mountains.

I tell him I have just spoken with one of his boys, Tom Callahan, who is now at the State Department. Callahan has given me a description of Bob I like.

"What did he say?" Bob asks.

"He said you are not a naturally born saint," I reply.

It is one of those pregnant sentences, full of meaning and depth, embracing at once where Bob is and where he has been, his compassionate present and his somewhat carefree and careless past—a time when even his sister Sheila describes Bob as reckless and restless, wild and free, full of life and burning the candle at both ends.

Bob laughs at Callahan's description. "He was one of our stars," he says and recalls missions Callahan, then an eager twenty-four-year-old looking for meaning and purpose, led into Ecuador, Sudan, and the Philippines.

"So where does it come from?" I say, asking the obvious question. "Who planted the seeds of giving?"

"I guess my Mom," Bob says. "She was always a crusader."

Bob's grandmother was a suffragette. As a result, his mother, Ella Conover Macauley, had always been socially conscious. She was a member of the Women's Christian Temperance Union and once considered running for public office. When the children were growing up, she became heavily involved in the overseas foster-parents program. From an early age, Bob and his two sisters—Connie, three years older, and Sheila, nine years younger—were instructed to send their old clothes and part of their allowances to foster siblings in places like Poland, Latvia, and Korea.

"The great constant in our lives was this backdrop

of Mother wrapping packages or clothes to send to children she wanted to help," Sheila recalls. "She was always helping people and adopting children around the world. She would show us photographs and tell us stories about their lives and what they had done with the money we sent. She was very personally involved."

"You'd come home and she'd be knitting a sweater," Bob recalls. "I'd say, 'Mom what are you doing? I have enough sweaters.' And she'd say, 'Oh no, this is for Boris in Romania' or some other child in China or Russia. She'd write to these people and tell them about our lives, freedom, and democracy, and send them the sweater or something else and a few bucks. After a while, it sort of infused itself into our way of life."

If Bob's charitable instincts were nursed by his mother, his enterprising nature came from his father Milton, as well as his penchant for rising early. None of the family can remember beating their father to the breakfast table. He was always in place by 6:00 AM.

Milton was a well-to-do paper broker and a self-made man. His father died while he was still young.

He went to work at the age of thirteen and only got as far as the sixth grade, educating himself by reading at night by candlelight.

He was straight and solid, a man who valued his integrity and worked hard. By 1919 his hard work had paid off and he was able to start his own company, M. L. Macauley and Co., in New York. A decade later when Bob was entering the second grade, he was doing well enough to send his son to a private school, Greenwich Country Day School.

Founding headmasters John L. Minor and George Meadows were the headmasters during Bob's time at Greenwich Country Day. Bob got to know them well due to his oft-requested presence in their offices for skipping school, not going to class, or one or another of his entrepreneurial antics.

Bob and his family didn't have a great deal of money, but they were comfortable. Most of the other kids in that school came from great wealth. This fact might have been a problem for someone else. For Bob, it was an opportunity.

"We used to go up to the Yale games sometimes and they would sell round pins with Army, Navy,

Yale, what have you," Bob recalls. "They would have a little ribbon and a football on them. We used to go out at recess and the kids would buy them from each other. I remember one kid came out with a Holy Cross button and the kids started to bid on it. One bid a dollar, another five. They were going crazy. I thought this would be like shooting fish in a barrel."

Bob got one of the pins and found a piece of cardboard on the reverse side saying where the pins were made, a store down on Park Row in New York. He got his father to lend him one of his salesmen as an escort and went down to the shop. He was pleased to find they had pins for every school he had ever heard of, from Sawatch Teachers to Podunk U. More important, he found they were selling the pins for a nickel each.

"The next day when we went out at recess I had them pinned to my sweater," Bob says. "Schools you'd never heard of before. The kids would say, 'Bob, I've got to have it.' They'd started out bidding at a dollar and sometimes would go up to five dollars. I did that for three days."

Bob's budding business came to an end when his father got a call from the headmaster saying his son had practically wiped out the whole school. Families were calling up and complaining, "Who is this guy Bob Macauley? My son in the fifth or sixth grade comes home and he wants to borrow five or ten dollars. When I ask him what he is going to do with this, he says he wants to buy more pins from Macauley."

Bob remembers he had made eighty dollars by the time they shut his venture down. But that didn't stop him from starting another. After trading pins, he developed a lively business reselling marbles he had won from his classmates and then branched out into selling for three cents apples he had acquired for two. He cleaned out his classmates enough times that the headmaster routinely posted himself at the door. As they headed out for recess, he would look for Bob, shake a finger at him, and remind him, "No business today."

At Andover Bob continued to be on intimate terms with his headmaster since he showed little interest in going to class and found dormitory life confining. Along with a couple of friends he built a treehouse on a pond a mile from school where he could stay up as late as he wanted and indulge his passion for the outdoors.

Bob also continued to refine his entrepreneurial instincts, starting his own laundry business. "When I went to Andover they had boxes so that you could send clothes home to get them washed by your mother or the maid and then returned to you. I thought this wasn't a very good way to do it. I made a deal with a guy in a neighboring town—I guess I was a freshman then. I would find the business and this man would do the laundry for a price instead of the kids sending them home for someone to do it there. I nearly cleaned out the school."

Since that went so well, Bob decided to set up a dry cleaning business. "I made a deal with Langrocks, a clothing store, that for every ten dry cleaning jobs I got them, they'd give me a suit," Bob recalls.

The headmaster at Andover at that time was Dr. Claude Fuess, a noted educator who once graced the cover of *Time* magazine. Fuess was a bald-headed man with a facial twitch. Bob had a standing date with him every Saturday at 8:20 AM. The dialogue between them was invariably the same. Dr. Fuess would open every session by saying, "Well, Macauley, did you get to any classes this week?" Bob would admit he hadn't and promise to do better next week.

"Fuess didn't go for me a bit," Bob says. "He kept saying he wished he could throw me out but my grades were too high."

His sister Sheila confirms Bob's recollection. "We were always going up to school to bail Bob out," she says.

But in the spring of 1941, there were other priorities. After Hitler had invaded Czechoslovakia and Poland, Bob saw the war coming and decided to run away and join the Canadian Air Force. The Saturday before he left, he broke the news to Dr. Fuess. When he heard Bob was leaving, Fuess responded with one word—"Good."

Ironically, more than fifty years later, Bob returned to Andover to receive the school's highest honor—an award named after Claude Fuess, a fact he still finds amusing. "Dr. Fuess must have rolled over in his grave," he says.

Not long after enrolling in Greenwich Country Day School, Bob joins a pickup game of football. As he pulls to make a block, someone comes busting through the line. The kid is about the same size as Bob, but leaner and faster. He hits Bob hard enough to knock his wind out.

It is his formal introduction to George Bush and the beginning of a lifelong friendship. They will be together through grammar school, prep school, and college. They will party together—"I met Barbara before George," Bob is quick to note—and play together, teaming up to play doubles during the summer tennis circuit and winning a number of club tournaments.

"He was captain of the baseball team," Bob recalls. "He played first base. He was a superb athlete and a good all-around player. I was a pitcher and a pretty good hitter. I liked the home run ball. I wouldn't always hit it, but when I did it went a long way."

It is worth noting that Bob never learned how to bunt. "Playing it safe never appealed to me," he says.

The only thing George and Bob didn't do together was study. George was a model student. While Bob got good grades, he never had much use for class and couldn't find the library at Andover when his father asked to see it.

Bush was a leader all the way through school. When George was sworn in, a reporter asked Bob if he was surprised his friend had been elected president. "I would have been more surprised if he hadn't," Bob responds. Meanwhile, Bob marched to his own drummer and took the road less traveled. "He was always a bit of a renegade," President Bush recalls. "He did everything his own way."

Two years after leaving office, George and Barbara Bush attend an AmeriCares gala in New Canaan, Connecticut. It is a fund raising event like no other. The site is an airplane hangar near Westchester Airport. Nearly a thousand people are gathered there to dine and dance. At 10:00 PM, the doors to the hangar open. Attendees are greeted with the sight of an AmeriCares charter plane set to depart on a relief mission to Guatemala.

As the crowd gathers to watch, fifty people in formal wear leave the party and walk down a red carpet to join the mercy flight. The Bushes lead the parade. They are followed by key donors, staff, and invited guests, my wife and I among them. The plane arrives in Guatemala City at 1:30 A.M. After a couple of hours of sleep and an opportunity to freshen up, the party gets a first-hand look at AmeriCares in action. Guatemala is one of the poorest countries in the Western hemisphere. AmeriCares has been providing assistance to the people here since 1984, delivering medicine and supplies to more than fifty indigenous organizations.

At 8:00 A.M. the party visits El Basurero, a large landfill on the outskirts of Guatemala City. Thousands of men, women, and children, the poorest of the poor, live here, fashioning shelters out of scraps of metal and picking through other people's garbage, looking for something to eat.

At 10:00 A.M. we visit the Sisters of Charity Home, where Mother Teresa's missionaries provide care for the elderly and disabled. At noon, before getting on the plane and heading back, we visit Mi Casa, an orphanage that fills a city block.

Angie and I are particularly taken with the orphanage. The children are beautiful, happy and well cared for. They call the director "Uncle John." When we are introduced, I ask him what support AmeriCares provides. Uncle John gives me a long list that includes many of the things we have brought with us. When I ask how long this has been going on, he catches me by surprise. "Bob helped set up this place," he says. As long as I have known Bob, I have never heard him mention Mi Casa. He seems to be everywhere.

Now with a reason and the opportunity, I ask him about his involvement.

"John worked for a bank," Bob explains. "He helped out with the Shoeshine Boys for a while and made seven or eight trips to Saigon for me. When we folded up that foundation, I asked him to come up and talk with me. We both wanted to do something for needy kids but the constraining influence is always the money. I didn't have the money and neither did he.

"I told him I would borrow the money to get something started, but first I said I wanted him to go around the world and figure out where we could save the most kids for the fewest bucks. He agreed to do that. I got him a ticket that was four pages long with stops all over Asia, Africa, and South America. When he came back, he said, 'Guatemala. I think we can leverage every dollar we get down there.' We started with four kids. He has leveraged that into the place you saw and 1,200 kids. It all started with 1,500 bucks of seed money Leila and I kicked in."

Snapshots

*A*t the age of twelve, Bob Macauley has his first
piano recital. He is scheduled to play "Rustles of
Spring" by the Norwegian composer, Christian
Sinding. The piece is written to be played entirely on the
black keys. As he begins, Bob's hand slips off D-sharp and
lands on D-natural instead.

Rather than back up and begin again, Bob pushes fore-
word. He plays the entire piece on the white keys, transpos-
ing as he goes. When he finishes, Bob looks up to see his
piano teacher, a portly woman named Mrs. Livingston,
nearly overcome with anxiety.

"How did you do that?" Mrs. Livingston asks.

"I don't know," Bob responds. "I just did it."

Neither of them knew until that moment that he had perfect pitch.

In the late fifties, a thirty-nine year-old Macauley is visiting his farm in upstate New York when a sudden storm sets in. Hurriedly, he gets his things together and heads home in what is by now a blizzard. He is driving a Lincoln Continental. The top is down because it will not go up. Snow is pouring in, filling the car and burying the driver as he makes his way back to Connecticut.

Somewhere along the way, Bob discovers that if he can get the car going fast enough the force of the wind against his windshield will lift the snow above his head and propel it behind him as he goes. He is doing seventy when a policeman stops him. Though he is exceeding the speed limit by forty miles an hour, he escapes a ticket by convincing the officer it was actually safer for him to drive at such speed under these circumstances.

"No ray of sunlight is ever lost,
but the green that it wakes needs time to sprout,
and it is not always granted to the sower
to see the harvest. All work that is worth anything
is done in faith."

ALBERT SCHWEITZER

Bob's Folly

*B*ob's least likely and perhaps most ambitious charity was his business. "To my mind there was no difference between my business interests and my philanthropy," Bob explains. "Virginia Fibre *was* my philanthropy. I wanted to make an economic and social impact in a depressed area."

From the beginning, Bob wanted it to be a business like no other. As he saw it, Virginia Fibre would be organized on Christian principles and guided by the ten commandments with a chaplain in a position of ultimate authority. The chaplain would serve as counselor and spiritual director for the employees and act as their ombudsman to top management. He would sit on the board of directors and have final authority on all personnel matters.

"In the area of human relations, we believe in the four absolutes enunciated in the Sermon on the Mount," the chaplain, Pastor Paul Sartorio, was quoted as saying. "They are absolute honesty, absolute purity, absolute unselfishness, absolute love."

Virginia Fibre was designed to be a people-oriented company based on mutual respect and trust. Everyone would be treated as an equal with a partnership interest. Everyone would have a stake in the company's success. The company's motto, Bob decreed, would be: "One for all and all for one."

Predictably perhaps, the *Wall Street Journal* dubbed the venture a failure before they broke ground. The *Journal* ran a front-page article calling the project "Bob's Folly." They said it would never work. They were very nearly right.

Following World War II, Bob entered Yale and earned a B.A. in international relations. By the time he graduated in 1949, he was on his way to Europe with a grant to study the recovery in Italy, Greece, and Turkey.

But within a week, Bob found himself bored with this activity and headed for Paris where he found a job playing piano. "I played in Paris, Brussels, Cannes, North Africa, all over," he says of those days. "I liked the hours—nine to midnight—which left the days free to chase girls, play golf, go sailing, and hit the casinos."

"He was a wild thing," Sheila recalls. "All over the place."

He says he was a good piano player, not a great one. Still, he was good enough to substitute for Eddie Duchin in his band once, and he could play anything. Once he heard a piece, he could play it from memory all the way through. Bob quickly learned he could make a pretty good dollar playing in the nightclubs and cocktail joints in Europe. But his salad days came to an end one night at the gaming tables in Cannes.

He had been living day-to-day, playing, partying, and gambling. Every night ended at the casinos. Characteristically, he swung for the fences and played the long odds, hoping for a big score. When he finally hit it, he knew it was time to move on. Bob chartered a yacht and cruised through his winnings, saying good-bye to his carefree lifestyle.

When the money was gone, he came home and joined his father's paper brokerage business. He did not like it at first, but soon learned he had a knack for the job. His affability and interest in people made him a natural. He made his customers his friends and became intimately involved in their lives. They rewarded him with their loyalty and their business.

When the Korean War came along, paper got scarce and Bob began doing quite well. He asked the company whose paper he sold to put him on straight commission and made $189,000 the first year. He was thirty-five years old.

"The next year they fired me," Bob says. "I was making three times as much as the president of the company."

Bob changed companies and the pattern repeated. Three more times he got fired for making too much money. Each time he was fired, the company tried to hold on to all the accounts Bob had created, betting the customer would be more loyal to the company that produced the paper than to the salesman who sold it. To their surprise, Bob kept 96 percent of his client base every time he moved.

His last employer was Great Northern Nekoosa. With his history in mind, they decided to buy him out rather than fire him. Great Northern bought Bob's company on the condition that he come with it. He was given the title of Vice President of Great Northern and an office in their executive suite.

"But he was never there," Mike Donovan, a long-time friend and business associate, recalls. "What they didn't understand is that Bob did his job externally. They were always after him to come to meetings. He could not work in that environment. He had owned his own company and was selling on commission. It was *his* company and *his* work hours, and *his* people worked the way they wanted to work as long as they got the job done."

Increasingly frustrated, Bob decided he needed his own paper company. His exposure to the corporate world convinced him that when he started this company he didn't want it to operate the way a normal corporation functions. In 1972 Bob made the decision to "go for it."

Charlie Chandler remembers getting a call from Bob in April of that year. Charlie had just been promoted from managing accounting at one of Great Northern's paper mills to a position as director of profit planning for the entire company. He had known and worked with Bob for years.

"I had just moved to the Stamford office," Chandler says. "My wife and son and I had just arrived in town. Our furniture was still in a van on its way up. We checked into the Howard Johnson's in Darien, Connecticut, and found the phone ringing when we walked into the room. It was Bob calling. He said he would like to come by and have breakfast in the morning."

Bob told Chandler he wanted to start his own company and build a paper mill in North Carolina or Virginia. "He said 'I need a good numbers guy to help me,'" Chandler remembers. "I said, 'Gee, Bob I just accepted a new position. The furniture isn't even here yet; let me think about it.'"

After thinking about it for a while, Chandler said, "Here's what I'll do. I'll work with you, I'll do the numbers, I'll do the forecast, but I won't quit my job. I'll do all that after hours and at night and we'll see how it works out."

Chandler did as he said he would for three months. Finally, it got to the point where he knew he had to do one or the other. Attracted by the adventure of building a new company, he quit Great Northern to work on Virginia Fibre.

"If there ever was a guy who will roll the dice every time, it's Bob," Chandler says. "Most of us are more conservative."

"What made you decide to roll the dice with him?" I ask.

"My confidence in him. I was confident in Bob's ability to make this project happen."

Chandler and Macauley developed a twenty-year pro forma and went calling on the moneymen. They called on every investment banker on Wall Street. "We wouldn't get too much beyond the fact that we wanted to borrow fifty million and didn't have much equity to put in," Chandler recalls. "Everybody would hear that and say, 'I'm sorry we can't help.'"

"Generally banks and insurance companies want

eighty percent equity and I had zero percent equity," Bob explains. "So it was a tough sell. When I started the company, they'd ask, 'How much are you going to put up?' I'd say zero and they'd throw us out."

The last investment banker they called on was at a company named White Weld. Their representative listened politely and said you cannot put together financing for that project here in New York City. If you are going to build a plant like this in North Carolina or Virginia it is going to be good for that part of the country so you need to go talk to a regional investment banker. The one he recommended was Jim Wheat of Wheat First Securities in Richmond, Virginia. He was a local investment banker with offices in Virginia and North Carolina. Plus, he was said to be well plugged in to government and Wall Street.

They left the office and went to the first pay phone they could find and made an appointment for the following Friday. On that day Macauley and Chandler went to Wheat's office in Virginia. When they met, they were surprised to find Wheat was blind.

"I look at Bob and he looks at me," Chandler recalls. "We didn't know what to expect. Wheat came around the desk and said, 'Good to see you guys. Come on in and have a seat.' He asked if we had a pro forma. I said, 'Yes, we have twenty years here.'"

Wheat told Chandler to start out with the first year and read the profit and loss statement and then read the source and application of funds and go through it from there.

"Probably the biggest chore I have ever had in my life," Chandler says, "was to read those twenty documents. Each page probably had twenty columns. I read them one by one while Wheat sat behind his desk with his head down, almost like he was asleep. After I finished reading all of the documents, Wheat sits up and says, 'Okay, let's see, over there in year seven we have the debt balance down to this, and over there in year so and so. . . .' He remembered in his mind's eye all of those documents and could talk intelligently about them from that point forward."

After they told their story, Wheat said, "This job is going to be as tough as a mule eating briars through a fence, but I think I can put it together for you if you will let me raise a little more equity."

Bob responded by saying he wanted to control the

company. "If I can't control the company, I might as well stay where I am."

"I didn't say you have to give up control, but we have to raise more equity. We need to have about six million in equity to raise forty-four."

"How am I going to maintain control?"

"Your stock will have more weight than the rest."

"That started the process," Chandler says. "Jim put together a financial package that allowed us to build the mill. It had every debt instrument you could think of—senior debt, junior debt, equipment supplier debt, subordinating debt, interest during construction added to debt. It had layer after layer after layer. The paper machine supplier took a note for the paper machine. Then there was subordinating debt—that was unsecured, that was just people hoping we would succeed."

Virginia Fibre closed on its financing package in October of 1973. There were forty people representing the various players with an interest in the mill seated at the table.

"Virginia Fibre is another shining example of Bob's salesmanship," Mike Donovan says. "Wheat said a number of times that until the day he died he would never understand why he did what he did for Bob. The financials were unbelievable. The location was different. The concept of everyone being part of the team and sharing in profits was a 180-degree turn from every other paper mill in the business. We had every obstacle you could imagine."

It is March of 1995. Out of the blue, Bob calls to invite me to come to Virginia Fibre. He is going to be there for a board meeting he thinks I may find interesting. It is a five-hour drive from Washington, past Charlottesville to Lynchburg, and then down a two-lane country road that ultimately leads to the mill.

As I drive on to the property, I am greeted with a sign announcing "Virginia Fibre: Partners in Progress." We are in the middle of nowhere, the kind of place where nothing changes from generation to generation and poverty is bone deep. It is hard to think in terms of progress.

I take a tour of the facility and have the rudiments of the business explained to me by Mike Giles, one of Virginia Fibre's officers. "It is a 175,000 ton-per-year pulp and paper mill," he says. *I don't know much about the business, but I know that's big.*

"Virginia Fibre produces the corrugated inside layer of cardboard," Giles said.

What is that?

"One of the components used to make a cardboard box."

Not the box?

"No, we sell to the people who make the box."

I had no idea a business of this size could be focused so finely. It's as if one of the great pyramids had been upended and was being supported on a plate.

After the tour, I have a chance to meet the other officers and some of the board members of Virginia Fibre. We have dinner and socialize a bit. The next morning I head home, not quite sure why I was there.

The day after I return home, FedEx delivers an uncharacteristically long letter from Bob. He says he must confess some ulterior motives in inviting me down to Lynchburg. "I wanted you to get a good look at both Virginia Fibre and AmeriCares, with the thought in mind that at some future date, you might give consideration to joining the Board of Directors of both Virginia Fibre and AmeriCares."

I am stunned.

"There was no spontaneity in my thinking," he contin-ues, "it has been with me for quite a long time. But before issuing such an invitation, I wanted you to get a good 'feel' of what we are all about at VFC. As I look back on VFC to 1972 when I first conjured up the idea of trying to build a large, integrated paper mill, my long-range plan was for a corporation to be a force for good, anywhere and everywhere in the world. Not only for our shareholders and our employ-ees, but with a pronounced accent on humanitarianism."

Virginia Fibre Corporation's Ten Commandments

1 Respect, to the utmost, the individual worth
and dignity of each and every employee.

2 Provide leadership in which all employees may
find faith and confidence.

3 Provide adequate training opportunities for all
employees, and encourage them to develop
their capacities to their maximum potential.

4 Make demonstrated ability the primary basis
for promotion, and wherever possible adhere
to the practice of promotion from within.

5 Provide fair and equitable compensation for all
employees by maintaining wage rates equal to

or better than the prevailing rates for comparable work for our industry in the area.

6 Promote the economic security of all employees by intelligent administration of a balanced program of company-paid employee benefits.

7 Provide facilities and working conditions which are considerate of the employee's health and safety.

8 Provide free and open channels of communication.

9 Guarantee that the personnel policies of our company, both in spirit and according to the letter, will be followed at all times.

10 Provide equal employment opportunity without regard to race, color, religion, sex, national origin, or age.

Signed:

       R. C. Macauley   Paul F. Sartario
         President   Chaplain

"Many times in a day I realize how much my outer and inner life is built upon the labors of my fellow-men, both the living and those now dead, and how earnestly I must exert myself, in order to give in return at least as much as I have received."

ALBERT EINSTEIN

Grace Under Pressure

*C*onstruction of the Virginia Fibre mill took twenty months. The first run was in August of 1975. Even then success did not come swiftly. "Bob's concept was that we were going to hire a skeletal number of people," Chandler recalls. "He said, 'They are not going to have any titles. We are not going to describe their responsibilities. They will all know what needs to be done and everybody is going to go do whatever needs to be done to get the job done.' That was his concept of partnership. As part of that he said if the company did well he wanted all employees to share in the profitability of the company. He said, 'I don't want the employees to worry about anything. We will pay for everything.'"

"Like I told Charlie when we had breakfast on the first of April 1972, I don't like working for a big company," Bob explains. "You get jerked around too much. Great Northern had all these rules, like their mandatory breakfast meeting, for example. They had a room in the J. P. Morgan Bank downstairs. You were supposed to be there every day at 8:30 to have breakfast. But you couldn't talk about work, just socialize. I said to hell with that. I used to get to the office at 5:30 anyway. All that red tape drove me crazy. You had to do this, you had to that. And there was no incentive for performance. I was paying salesmen who worked for me a hundred grand. The president of the company only made $78,000."

Still, Bob's "partnership in progress" took a while to evolve. "We went through three mill managers before we could operate this partnership the way we wanted to," Chandler says. "But from day one, we paid for all the benefits and the structure to allow employees to participate in profitability started early on. Bob said he didn't want a company where there is a union, where there is a bureaucracy, where there are workers and non-workers. He said we want a small group of people who are here to build a new kind of company."

"I had been at so many meetings in large corporations where you had a rectangular table," Bob says. "Labor sat on one side and management on the other. I said screw that. We are not going to do that. We are going to have a round table and we will all mix in. We never had an employee. We only had partners. Everyone shared with a percentage based on productivity—not money the company made or lost—because the guys in the mill had no concept of what that was. They couldn't influence your selling price. The only thing they could do was make more paper and better paper.

"We paid higher than average salaries, but we always had the lowest labor costs. Competitors would ask: 'How are you doing this?' It's simple. People work harder when they have an incentive," Bob explains.

The men and women at Virginia Fibre embraced the partnership concept quickly and completely. Even in the beginning, Virginia Fibre's bonus checks would sometimes run $5,000 to 10,000 above salary. Such was their commitment to the company that when interest rates rose and Virginia Fibre was having a tough time refinancing its debt, a delegation was sent to see Bob.

"They handed me all these checks," he says. "There were about thirty of them. They said, 'These are our incentive compensation checks. We want to give them back to you.' I took all of them because we needed the money pretty bad at the time and that kept us running for two days, but when the market turned I paid them back every dollar with interest at the prime rate."

With one thing after another, Virginia Fibre skirted default for years. "The first five years were awful," Chandler says. "The first year the problems were in production. After that it was debt burden. We had every problem you could have except labor problems. We never had labor problems."

"During the first couple months we were making paper with an awful smell. Twenty-five days into the plant operation the phone in the guest house where I was staying rang at two in the morning," Bob remembers. "All I heard was the sound of someone retching. It was a neighbor thirty-five miles away. The stench had gotten so bad we were wrecking the whole community. At one point, we had more product coming back than going out.

"We were two to three days from going bankrupt, and we had to do something."

"I'd say it was more like minutes," Frank Louthan, a member of Virginia Fibre's board, recalls. "The plant was on the verge of being closed down. The paper it was making was low quality. We had no volume and it stunk. That's enough to run anybody out of town. Everyone else was ready to cut and run, but Bob was unflappable."

When Bob's children were growing up, he made signs to guide them. One of his favorites was GUP. "When they asked Aristotle to define courage," Bob explains, "he asked for a year to think about it. When they came back, he said, it's 'grace under pressure.'"

Louthan still speaks of Macauley's grace under pressure with admiration. "To solve a crisis is one thing, but to be unflappable in a crisis for several days and weeks at a time is something else," he says. "From that time on, I was a staunch supporter and believer in him."

Bob found the answer to his production problem thanks to one of his competitors.

"We found there was another mill in Paris, Texas, run by Weyerhaeuser that had the same structural configuration as we did," he says, "so I called up the president of the company and asked if I could bring my people down to talk with his people. We chartered a plane on my Diner's Card because we were flat out of money."

Bob rented a barn, brought a case of Johnny Walker and a keg of beer, and closed the men inside to hash it out. "Every couple of hours, I would stick my head in and ask, 'Have you found it yet? What are we doing wrong?' Finally, about one in the morning one of my men came running out and said, 'We've found it, Bob.'"

The second-stage washing was using a condensate from the previous washing instead of fresh river water. The solution was simple. "All they had to do was switch it," he says. "One phone call from the plane solved it."

"Every week there was one of these kinds of things. Once we got the production problem solved, market prices fell, interest rates went up to 20%, all of our senior debt was floating interest—2½ points over prime—so we were paying interest on huge amounts of debt at 22.5%. That was just killing us. You had no dough; you didn't know what to do. I'd call the banks and beg for one more week and tell them, 'We are going to make it; we are going to make it.' And they'd say, 'Okay, but next time we are going to melt the machine down.' Next week, I'd get on the phone again and plead for one more week.

"But we never had people quit. Everybody was a partner. Everybody was equal. We were all in it together. We knew if we couldn't pull it off, the banks would take it over and we were all out of a job.

"The same with our suppliers. If you run out of wood, you are out of business. The bankers kept saying, 'What are you going to do about the woodlands?' Paper companies will go out and buy millions of acres. It would have cost us half a billion dollars. We had used everything we had on the machinery. We didn't have enough money to buy one acre. So we came up with the Land Owners Assistance Plan.

"We identified all the landowners within fifty miles. We made them partners. We'd go to Mrs. Smith who might own twenty-five acres and ask for an option for the wood on her land at the market price whenever we needed it. And if we needed her lumber, we told her we would replant her land with pine. A lot of the landowners felt it was almost too good to be true. We tied up all the land within fifty miles without paying a nickel. We had so much wood we went out and sold wood to other mills that didn't have any. Sometimes we made more money on the wood than on the paper. Everybody made out."

"Where did your concept of partnership come from?" I ask.

"Sharing the wealth is part of our responsibility," Bob replied. "I always thought this way, even when I was working for Great Northern. We are all equal. We are all God's children. We treat them as partners and expect them to act like partners

"Paper is the fifth biggest industry in the country, so it is pretty cutthroat. But I always felt if you were fair to your people, they would return the favor by working harder for you. Be fair to your fellow man and they will treat you well. Virginia Fibre became like a family. If we had 200 guys on a shift and three weren't pulling their weight, I didn't have to worry about it. The others would straighten them out because the loafers were getting into their pockets. Everyone gets less if one guy isn't doing his job. It became self-policing and self-correcting. All for one and one for all.

"The partnership philosophy is the opposite of exploitation. In a partnership, if you are labor, I'm a foreman; I'm not trying to exploit you and get you down on the pay. I'm trying to give you an incentive to work harder. The reason we had such low labor cost is because the guys worked so hard. I'd see guys punch out, put the time card back in, and go back to work."

Finally, in 1985, with its debt load much reduced, Virginia Fibre made $8 million on sales of $60 million. "At that point," Bob says, "I knew I could finally do pretty much what I wanted."

For Bob that meant giving back.

"It's part of Bob's basic principles to help the little man," Chandler says. "So he brought it up to the board, saying we have a lot to be thankful for with this company. We started out with nothing. We've seen some hard times. Now we are doing well. We need some pay back. The board passed a resolution for the company to give ten percent of pretax profits to charity—one percent stayed in the local area and nine percent would go to AmeriCares. That continued until Greif Brothers acquired us. Greif is a publicly-owned company and couldn't do that with the stockholders' money."

When I visited Virginia Fibre, I was impressed with the fact that people in a rural community were so involved in the world. "How did that happen?" I ask Chandler.

"In order to accomplish what Bob wanted for that company, you had to have open communications— I mean completely open," he said. "This was just part of that. When Bob started AmeriCares and we started supporting it, people were told about it. People were kept up-to-date on airlifts and Virginia Fibre's contributions. In order to help bring Virginia Fibre and AmeriCares together, Bob offered people trips on airlifts. It just brought us close together. Even today the mill people still feel a close relationship. Everybody took pride in what AmeriCares was doing and what they were helping to make possible."

"You know him as well as anyone," I said. "What makes him tick?"

"I remember having dinner with him one time and Bob's sister was there. We were talking about Bob and I said, 'Have you noticed that wherever Bob is there is a little bit of chaos or confusion? People are running beyond their capacity and doing more than they think they can do.'

"She said he has always been that way. When they were young she said the rest of them would be sitting around reading and everything would be quiet and under control. Then the back door would bust open and here comes little Bob. Within three minutes of him coming in the room, there was mass confusion. Everyone was going everywhere. Wherever he is, he has five or six things on his mind and he wants five or six people to do this or that. It's just Bob.

"Most of us deal in a world of reality of what I can do and what I can accomplish and what I can influence. In Bob's world there's nothing that can't be done. There's nothing that he thinks he can't influence. He thinks if you want to bad enough, and try hard enough, you can make it happen. There is no limit in his world to what can be accomplished. If you look at some of the things he has done, he demonstrates that. His thinking is so far beyond the rest of us in what we think is possible. Who else would have said I am going to build a fifty million dollar business out of nothing?

"To me, I know right off the bat that can't be done, so I don't try to do it. But to Bob there is no such thing as it cannot be done. There were so many occasions when I told Bob that just can't be done. Guess, what? He did it. There is something special about Bob. There's no limit to what he can accomplish. And what is scary is that it starts to rub off. Often now I say something and my wife will say, 'You are beginning to sound like Macauley again.'"

After talking with Chandler, I called Bob to get his reaction. "Chandler says you do more than make things happen," I said. "He says you deliberately stir things up."

"Absolutely," Bob responds, "that's the only way you solve anything. You've got to shake things up—as Charlie well knew. Charlie gave up a good job and security. He had just moved his wife up north. He was the only one who knew how bad it was sometimes. It was one fire after another. Every day."

"Is your philosophy part of the ancient Chinese tradition that in chaos there is opportunity?" I ask.

"I think sometimes you have got to create the chaos to get the opportunity. It sort of happens that way. I guess it is a perverse way of being, but I love challenges. It gets me going. It's part of my mindset. You get so accustomed to facing challenges and winning. If you don't have one every week or so, you wonder what you're doing. Every problem is an opportunity."

"Are you saying it's a way of pushing yourself?"

"I think you have to make very, very high demands on yourself. You swing for the fences. Don't bunt. That was one of my slogans. Go for the home run ball."

"Are you always taking chances?"

"I think you have to. Big risk, big reward. What

were the chances of Virginia Fibre? It was folly. Nobody could have a company like this, all debt, no equity, the ten commandments. It really was folly all the way through—except it worked. Same with AmeriCares. Whoever would have thought that it could have grown to where it is now?"

"I am a link in a chain, a bond of connection between persons. He has not created me for naught. I shall do good. I shall do His work. I shall be an angel of peace; a preacher of the truth in my own place while not intending it—if I do but keep His Commandments."

JOHN HENRY CARDINAL NEWMAN

A Grateful Heart

fter college, Bob considered converting to Catholicism. Bishop J. Fulton Sheen, then a monsignor, provided private instruction. "He had three private pupils," Bob recalls, "Henry Ford, Claire Booth Luce, and me. We came in every Saturday afternoon for more than a year. After that time when I still had reservations, he told me that the only way I would get it was to go to a monastery and live with the monks for a while."

Following Bishop Sheen's suggestion, Bob went to Sicily and lived in a monastery for several months. While he was there he made friends with a waiter named Giacomo.

At that time, work was still short in Italy. People shared jobs. Giacomo had seven kids. He worked three days—

*Monday, Wednesday, and Friday—leaving the job for some-
one else the rest of the week.*

*Above the monastery was an old church where Bob used
to retreat and meditate. There was an organ in the church
so old there were no white keys. Despite the fact that all the
ivory was gone, Bob found himself going there often to play.
It was a beautiful place high above the Mediterranean.*

*When he realized he wasn't going to make it and that
his issues with the church could not be resolved, Bob said
good-bye and went up to play the organ one last time before
he left. When he came out he found Giacomo waiting on
the steps.*

*Giacomo said he had heard Bob was leaving. He wanted
to express his affection and say a private good-bye. They
talked on the way down the mountain. Bob said he would
be leaving that evening and asked what Giacomo was going
to do that night. Giacomo said he would have his seven children, his mother and father, and his wife's mother and
father with him, but he didn't know what he was going to
do for dinner.*

*"My first thought was to offer him some money, then I
realized that would ruin our friendship," Bob says. "I said
'You must be terribly unhappy—going home to all these*

people and no way to feed them.' Giacomo stopped on the crooked path we were taking down the mountain and looked at me very seriously.

" 'Oh no,' he said. 'It would be a sin for me to be unhappy. That would be the core ingrato—the ungrateful heart. I have you as my friend. I have the sea and the pines and my family. I cannot be ungrateful for all the things God has given me.' Giacomo taught me a lesson I never forgot."

"Is that still the cardinal sin in your mind?" I ask.

"I think so, when you think of all the reasons we have to be happy. God has blessed me so much," Bob says and casts an eye toward his wife, "particularly in my marriage, if Leila will allow me to say so. A lot of good has come my way. I think of the success I have had in life, the things I have been able to do, the friendships I have had with Mother Teresa, George Bush, Peter Grace, Jim Wheat, and so many others. It is way beyond anybody's expectations. Certainly, my own. I never want to have an ungrateful heart."

The Dust of Life

On August 3, 1970, the *New York Times* ran a story about a man named Dick Hughes. Hughes was a conscientious objector to the Vietnam War. Instead of protesting or heading for Canada as many others did, he went to Vietnam on his own, using a press visa. He wanted to see what was happening there and do some kind of humanitarian work. He was drawn to the growing number of Vietnamese orphans, many the sons and daughters of American GIs, who were surviving on the street any way they could. They were called *bui doi*—the dust of life.

The *Times* article focused on one of these children—an eleven-year-old boy named Vo Van Be. He and his two little sisters were said to be among 130 children Hughes had rescued from the streets. They lived in an outdoor market for years, sleeping where they could before he came along. Now Vo struggled to support his young family shining shoes, while Hughes desperately sought support to keep his makeshift shelters going.

"In the United States people don't care anymore," Hughes was quoted as saying. "They want to forget about Vietnam and kids like these." The only American support he had received, he went on to say, was $50 from a general and a television set given to him by three women whose husbands were high-ranking members of the U.S. mission.

"I read his story and thought this guy is doing a wonderful thing," Bob recalls. "I got the author, Gloria Emerson, on the phone and I said I don't know where I am going to get it, but I am inclined to make a substantial donation to help. I asked her how I could contact Hughes and she told me.

"Hughes said he didn't have a lot of money and urgently needed $5,000. At that time, $5,000 was a lot of money for us. Leila and I had that much ear-marked for a new car. We talked about it and had an election—closed ballot. The whole family voted. We could either give the money to those kids in Vietnam or buy a new car. The vote was unanimous."

Macauley's gift became the seed money for what came to be known as the Shoeshine Boys Foundation, which provided a focus for the charitable urges Bob had retained from childhood. The Foundation, which drew its name from the only way Vo and many other orphans had to make an honest living, was headquartered in Bob's office in New York.

It was slow going at first, Bob remembers, but ultimately proved to be a great success after Young & Rubicam developed a striking pro bono ad campaign. Full-page ads placed in *Time*, *Life*, and other national publications of the day displayed an image of a man carrying a child with the headline, "He is not heavy. He is my brother." The ad invited people to help Dick Hughes and gave the address of the Shoeshine Boys Foundation.

Dick Hughes became celebrated enough that Ralph Edwards invited him back to the United States to do a segment on "This Is Your Life." As chairman of the Foundation, Bob was prominently featured on the program, but he had to promise not to use the occasion to ask for money. Bob kept his word but, to Edwards' chagrin, halfway through the show he unbuttoned his jacket and displayed a red sash around his middle marked with the Foundation's post office box in New York. He said nothing about it, and he didn't have to.

The program ran on Thanksgiving Day. The response was so strong Bob had to call in five operators to field the calls. From that point, money flowed into the Shoeshine Boys Foundation. The outpouring of gifts helped create fourteen homes that provided shelter for 2,500 children by war's end.

On April 4, 1975, a C5A Galaxy cargo plane took off from Saigon. There were 243 Vietnamese orphans on board, along with their escorts and a number of Air Force personnel.

It was less than a month before Saigon would fall. As North Vietnamese troops began to spread through South Vietnam, thousands of desperate, frightened people began pouring out of the country. The streets were mobbed with panicked Vietnamese people anxious to escape.

Over the next six months, 133,000 Vietnamese sought refuge in the United States. The children in the C5A hoped to be among them.

A row of two-foot-square cardboard boxes ran down the center of the plane. Each box contained a precious cargo of two or three infants. A long strap running the length of the plane stretched over the boxes to keep them in place. Toddlers and older children filled hard aluminum benches on each side of the aircraft.

Forty miles out of Saigon, an explosion blew off the rear door of the giant aircraft. The flight controls were crippled. Decompression filled the plane with fog and debris.

Somehow, the pilots managed to turn the plane around and head back to Saigon. The damaged plane crashed two miles from Tan Son Nhut airport. It skidded about 1,000 feet, bounced up in the air for half a mile, hit a dike, and shattered into a hundred pieces. Half of the passengers on board were killed immediately, including almost everyone in the bottom cargo compartment—mostly children two years of age and younger. Many of the survivors were critically injured and desperately in need of medical attention.

A lot of the children on this flight were Bob's kids. When he heard the news, he contacted the Pentagon and asked what was happening. He was told the military would be unable to fly the survivors to the United States for ten days.

"Once Bob gets the bit in his teeth, you can't take him off it," Prescott Bush recalls. "He couldn't bear the thought of those kids stranded over there. Who knew what would happen to them?"

"Many would have died," Bob says. "We could not wait."

Determined to get those babies out, Bob began calling airlines looking for a plane he could charter. Finally, he found one. Pan Am had a Boeing 747 in Guam they could send immediately to Saigon to transport the children. They said they would have to pull it out of a commercial run, so the cost would be steep—$251,000. They wanted ten percent down, the rest when the plane landed in San Francisco.

"No problem," Bob said and promised to put a check in the mail. He didn't bother to tell them he didn't have that kind of money at the time. His two-year-old business was still running in the red and soaking up all his resources.

"This all happened on a Friday," he explains. "By the time Pan Am got the check, I knew it would be Monday. I figured the kids would be safe by then, and we could worry

about the rest later."

Sure enough, on Sunday morning Pan Am called to say the plane was on its way, and they wanted the balance due. Bob cheerfully wrote them another check and sent it bouncing along. By the time a somewhat agitated Pan Am employee called to find out what was going on, Bob had taken out a loan against his house in New Canaan to cover the cost of his first mercy flight.

When Bob came home that evening, he found Leila waiting on the front porch. "The reporters were here," she said dryly.

"What did you tell them?" Bob asked.

She said, "I told them it sounded like a pretty good deal. Bob got the kids, and the bank got the house."

"You know, a lot of people have asked me how I do it," Bob adds almost as an afterthought. "It's really pretty simple. You get an airplane, fly over there, load up the kids, and go. It's pretty simple. You just have to have the balls to do it."

"I emphasized to Father Ryan my own deep conviction that it is woman who leads man out of his isolation. This she does by teaching him how to love. Through her, he learns what it means to be loved and to love; and such an experience is ultimately 'ecstatic.' It carries him beyond the barriers of self into a wider world where he meets his truest love, who is 'the mountains, the solitary wooded valleys, strange islands—and silent thoughts.' Woman leads man to an enlightenment where he loses his little self to find his true self, the universe of God."

ROBERT C. MACAULEY, JULY 28, 1964,
NOTES ON A PLANE TO NEW YORK
AFTER MEETING WITH
FATHER RYAN IN LONDON

Love Loves

*I*t's hard to talk about Bob without talking about Leila. They were married on the 29th of July 1965, twenty years to the day from the first time they went out and the first time he proposed.

Leila Lindgren was a war widow, working for Eastern Airlines when they met. Her first husband had been in the Air Force. She was a bride, a mother, and a widow within fourteen months. She was unquestionably the most beautiful woman Bob had ever seen. He was fresh out of the service, jobless, and looking for a good time, playing piano in Miami's nightspots to make ends meet.

For their first date, Bob took her to a place called Baker's. He only had a buck, he recalls, but beer at Baker's was only a quarter. Two beers later and fifty cents short of embarrassment, Bob began trying to talk her into going to a place where they could get a good steak—thinking of the place where he worked and knew he could run a tab. Leila wasn't sure why they couldn't eat where they were but amiably went along.

"We went down there and had a drink," Bob says. "It is a piano bar, and I am the guy who plays the piano. Pretty soon the boss starts giving me the eye. So I say, 'Would you like to hear me play the piano?' She says, 'No.' After a while I try again, and she says, 'Yes.'"

On the way home, Leila said, "You work there, don't you?"

Bob admitted he did but didn't tell her that was his primary source of income.

When they arrived, her father, a big Swede, noted they were a few minutes late and looked at Bob in a way that showed his displeasure. Before he could say anything more, Bob made an announcement.

"Mr. Lindgren," he said, "I am going to marry your daughter."

Taken somewhat aback, Leila's father asked, "How long have you known her?"

"Almost five hours," Bob said. "Not quite."

St. Augustine wrote, "Lord, help me to be good, but not just yet." Bob must have known what he meant. In his own words, he drank deeply from the pool of life. He was madly in love with Leila. She was equally smitten with him but wary of his hard-living ways. They both knew it would be a while before he was ready to settle down.

With that knowledge, Leila declined his proposal for the moment. "He was handsome and charming and impetuous but not very stable," she says.

Two years after they met, Bob went back to school. He graduated from Yale in 1949, but by graduation day he was already in Europe. He was back and forth playing piano abroad and working for his dad for years. Whenever he could, he would drive down to see Leila.

Finally, Bob said he was ready to settle down. He sent Leila a twenty-three page letter making his case.

Among other things, he told her that he would quit drinking if she would agree to marry him. She said if he did, she would. Bob stopped drinking cold turkey and never touched a drop again.

"Is she the person who has had the greatest influence on you?" I ask.

"If you take all the other people who have had an influence on me and rolled them all together, they wouldn't be half of what she has been. I was very much a bum before I got married. I kept all the whiskey companies going. I didn't live a very saintly life. I didn't do too much good. She has been my moral compass. She is the most intelligent person I have ever met. I just adore her, but she's a stern taskmaster. When she gets her jaw set and gets that look in her eye, you know that whatever she wants to happen is going to happen."

"I remember when I was single we often talked about marriage," I said. "You always told me, 'Don't settle.'"

"That's right. It never works. The chemistry is so important. You can't gradually evolve into it. You know. It is like a punch to the heart. This is the one.

People delude themselves by thinking you can grow into it. It doesn't work that way."

Snapshots

*I*n 1996, hatred flares up and burns African-American churches throughout the southern part of the United States. When the thirty-second church is burned, Macauley calls a press conference and announces he will rebuild every church that is burned down.

Immediately after the press conference, Macauley calls the chairman of Sprung Instant Structures, a Canadian company that manufactures modular structures and tells him what has happened. In 1991 Sprung had donated field hospitals and relief camps for Kurdish refugees escaping Iran. They are quick to sign on, agreeing to donate prefabricated churches to communities terrorized by arsonists.

Another church is burned the Wednesday after Bob's press conference. The next morning, the pastor calls Ameri-Cares looking for help. AmeriCares responds by picking up the material in Calgary, flying it down to the States, and building a new church in time for services on Sunday. Within days a place of worship stands where ashes once lay.

Understanding the importance of music in black congregations, Macauley is not content to rest there. Characteristically, he takes the extra step. He organizes something he calls "a piano lift," flying thirty-five pianos down south, one for each of the rebuilt churches.

Bob smiles when I ask about the pianos. "Always go a layer deeper," he says. "That's where the fun is."

"To be a man is, precisely, to be responsible.
It is to feel shame at the sight of what seems to be
unmerited misery.
It is to take pride in victory won by one's comrades.
It is to feel, when setting one's stone,
that one is contributing to the building of the world."

ANTOINE DE SAINT EXUPÉRY

How Wide Is Your Embrace?

*B*ob met Father Bruce Ritter in 1977 after he read an article in the *Daily News* about Covenant House. Leila had found the article and pressed Bob to read it, thinking he needed something to do after the Shoeshine Boys Foundation was dissolved. Ritter was operating out of a storefront, providing shelter and counseling for runaway kids in New York's Times Square. Ritter was doing good work by all accounts, but Covenant House was about to close its doors for lack of support.

At first, Ritter was reluctant to accept Macauley's invitation to come up to Connecticut. He didn't know Bob and thought it would be a waste of his time.

"There were so many children who needed help," Ritter would later say, "and we were facing bankruptcy." As much in desperation as interest, he made the journey.

Ritter, a man of tremendous intellect, had a doctorate in theology from Rome and a real sense of mission. The two bonded immediately and became fast friends. Bob persuaded a friend to pay off the debt that threatened Covenant House and joined the Board of Directors. Later he would serve two terms as chairman.

"Bob really made Covenant House," Chris Bell, an early associate of Ritter, remembers. "Through his magic and connections and influence and sheer will, he took what was a bankrupt agency and turned it around. It wouldn't have been possible without Bob."

Under Bob's guidance, Covenant House went from contributions of $400,000 in 1977 to $90 million a decade later. Covenant House grew from one center in New York to nine homes around the world, serving 123,000 kids. The mailing list had gone from 20,000 to over a million.

Covenant House achieved enough success that President Reagan invited Father Ritter to come down and sit in the balcony for his third State of the Union address and acknowledged his effort. Almost inevitably, it now seems, failure followed success.

Ritter was forced to resign from Covenant House in 1990 after several male runaways accused him of sexual misconduct. "Everyone abandoned Bruce in a matter of minutes," Bell recalls. "Not even days. It was hours. And we are talking about his order, his board, and his so-called best friends. They all abandoned him. And the press was having a wonderful time."

Bob didn't believe the charges against Father Ritter then, and he doesn't believe them now. He pushed Ritter to fight. When that proved untenable after his order forced him to resign, he fought the Board of Directors to see that Bruce got a stipend or some severance pay and found a place for him to stay.

"He is the real deal," Bell says. "When Bob is your friend, nothing shakes that. He loved the man before things blew up, and he loved the same man after. He was the only male friend in power who stuck by him."

Disavowed and disgraced, Ritter found a place in upstate New York. It was near a small town, but the rumors had reached even there. He was shunned and ostracized. No one would speak to him when he went out to buy a paper or walk his dog. He died alone a few years later.

"There were only twenty people at Bruce's funeral," Jim Schaeffer, another early associate of Ritter at Covenant House, recalls. "Bob and Leila were among them. Bob was in a wheelchair. He had no business being there. But he was there, front and center."

"They recognized each other's best qualities," Bell says. "Ritter had a tremendous sense of his mission— to help kids. His whole focus was to bring life and foundation to kids on the fringe of society, kids beaten up, murdered, and completely rejected by society because they were prostitutes. Bob saw Ritter's commitment as a great strength. Bob was selfless when I met him, but his relationship with Bruce brought it out more. He could have been spending his time and talents building corporations and making all kinds of money. Instead, he chose to spend his time helping kids no one else wanted to help. If I didn't know better, I would have thought Bob worked for Covenant House more than Virginia Fibre.

I asked Chris Bell the same question I had asked Chandler: What motivates him?

"I've never asked that question," he replied, "but I've always thought Bob was motivated by a feeling that he owes a debt to God."

"Absolutely," Bob said when I reported my conversation with Bell. "I have been uniquely blessed. From those to whom much is given, much is expected. I've felt that way from way back."

A Photo History

The birth of AmeriCares, September 13, 1981. "Can you do something to help the poor people of Poland?" Pope John Paul II asks.

"I don't impress easily," former President Bush said, "but I have to say I am in awe of Bob Macauley and what he has done with AmeriCares."

"Bob's office is painted a peaceful forest green. Bob sits at a massive desk facing an oversized leather chair. Pastoral paintings and candid photos of his wife and two children, a number of images of the Pope and Mother Teresa decorate the walls."

"Get the trucks, Bub," Mother Teresa said.

"Bob and Leila were married on the 29th of July 1965, twenty years to the day from the first time they went out and the first time he proposed."

Bob Macauley on an AmeriCares relief mission to Sarajevo in 1993.

Each year, Camp AmeriKids provides a traditional camping experience for 230 children ages 7 to 15 who are infected with or affected by HIV/AIDS.

Organized in 1988, AmeriCares HomeFront provides intense repairs for homeowners in need. Last year, 7,000 HomeFront volunteers were mobilized to repair 108 homes.

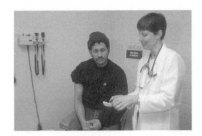
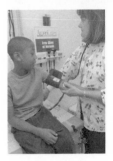

AmeriCares free clinics provide health care for people without
health insurance in Norwalk, Danbury, and Bridgeport, Conn.
Nearly 500 volunteer doctors, nurses, nonmedical volunteers and
interpreters have provided over $9 million in care over the last
ten years.

In presenting Bob with the President's Volunteer Action Award for AmeriCares, President Reagan noted AmeriCares had provided 165,000 pounds of chocolate to the children of Poland as part of their relief effort. "Next time you go to Poland," President Reagan said, "you may want to take a dentist along."

Bob and Leila Macauley with their son, Robert, at the presentation ceremony for the Albert Schweitzer Award.

Within a month of the tsunami in Southeast Asia, AmeriCares
delivered 155 tons of aid into the devastated areas of India,
Indonesia, and Sri Lanka where these children were found.
(Photo by Dr. Roddy Tempest.)

Last year, more than a million people were driven from their homes by a brutal civil war in the Darfur region of Sudan. AmeriCares responded by providing twenty-seven tons of relief supplies for Sudanese refugees, including those at the triage center above.

Curt Welling, President and CEO of AmeriCares, with refugees in Darfur.

Bob's World

*T*he first time I met Bob I asked him to describe what he did. He surprised me by saying, "I'm just a beggar. That's all I do. But I learned from the best— Mother Teresa."

A few years before, Bob and Mother Teresa had been on a flight to provide help to a children's home in Mexico City, Mexico. They were seated side by side, this powerful but small lady and this massive man in the coach section of a regional jet with about a hundred other passengers.

Shortly after the flight took off, the cabin attendants began meal service. When the attendant came to Mother Teresa she held up her hand.

"How much does this meal cost?" she asked.

The attendant said she didn't know exactly but probably about $1 American.

Mother said, "If I don't eat the meal, can I have the money for the poor?"

Surprised, the attendant did not know how to respond. She said she would have to ask someone. Dutifully, the woman went forward and reported Mother Teresa's request to the pilot who then contacted the company representative on the ground.

In a few minutes, the attendant returned. "Yes, Mother, you may have the money for the poor," she said.

Mother Teresa smiled and returned her tray. Bob immediately followed her example and handed his tray back as well. In short order, everyone on the plane followed suit, giving up their meals for people who needed it more.

"I thought we had done pretty well," Bob said, "and I told her so as we landed. We had made $129."

"She said, 'Get the food, Bub.' (She never could pronounce 'Bob.')

"I asked her what she meant, and she said, 'The airline can't use the food now. Let's get it so we can take it to the poor.'"

With some reluctance, Bob approached the airline officials there to greet the plane and repeated Mother Teresa's request. To his surprise, they readily agreed. But Mother was not satisfied.

When he returned with the happy news, she just looked at him and said, "Get the trucks, Bub. We can't deliver the food without the trucks."

"I couldn't beg for anything for myself," Bob says. "Even when I had no money and I was borrowing everything, I still wouldn't do it for myself. But if you are asking for someone else, it's different. I learned that from Mother Teresa."

Bob's quick response to the Pope's request in 1981 was the verbal equivalent of the bad check he had given Pan Am six years before. Only this time, he didn't know how he was going to cover it.

"I didn't know anything about medicine. We had no money. We were at ground zero," Bob recalls.

His first thought was to approach local pharmacies and ask for help. At the end of the first day all he had to show for it was $21 worth of medicine—a carton of aspirin and another carton of Unguentine.

Convinced that collecting supplies one carton at a time was not going to work, he decided he had to find a better way. Gathering the annual reports of the country's fifty largest pharmaceutical companies, Bob enlisted the assistance of two friends from his days at Covenant House—Peter Grace, chairman of W. R. Grace & Company, and Bill Simon, former Secretary of the Treasury. They sat down together and soon discovered they collectively knew someone on the boards of forty-seven of the fifty companies. The three men began working the phones. A few months later, more than 85,000 pounds of medical supplies worth $1.4 million had been donated and shipped to Poland.

"At AmeriCares, we do not believe that we can cure all of the ills of this world," Bob wrote in setting out the charity's aims in its first brochure, "but we believe that by acting as a pacesetter in sending supplies to disaster areas, we can lead the way."

Six years later Bob's solo humanitarian effort had evolved into the world's largest private relief organization. Two years after that, AmeriCares was named *Money Magazine*'s best charity with 99.1 percent of income spent on its programs.

By October 2000 when President Bush addressed the audience at that year's gala, AmeriCares had passed the two billion dollar mark. The three billion milestone followed three years later in October of 2003, four billion in 2004, and five in 2005.

As unique as what has been done is how it was done. "We were very small in the beginning," Terry Tarnowski, AmeriCares first employee, recalls. "One room. I was the only employee. Everyone else was just volunteering. Within months we had six or seven volunteers in that one room."

"There were never any meetings. We would go into Bob's office and say, 'Okay, what are we going to do?' We'd say, 'Let's do this,' and that was that. We might see each other and say, 'How is it going?' but there was never a question of a meeting tomorrow at 9:00 AM. In fifteen years at AmeriCares, I never heard of such a thing. Everyone knew what they were supposed to do, and they just did it."

Over lunch at the Hawk and Dove, a Capital Hill dive favored by congressional aides, I asked Tom Callahan to describe Bob's management style. Callahan drew a circle and put a dot in the center. "That's Bob," he said, pointing to the dot.

Jim Schaeffer, who became AmeriCares second

employee after leaving Covenant House, agreed. "Titles meant nothing. It didn't matter what your title was. It was a family. Everyone just did what needed to be done."

"You choose your people well, then give up the responsibility, and let them do their own thing," Bob explains. "When you charge them with the responsibility, you let them know you are not going to be there every five minutes telling them what to do or how to do it. You tell them, take a whack at the ball and hope they hit a home run. If you have chosen your people well, denying them the opportunity of sharing in the experience would be unfair to them. Whatever they do, they have to know you are behind them all the way."

"When Bob says, 'Make it happen. Just go out and do it,'" Callahan says, "and he sends a 23-year-old out to do something that is sensitive, could be dangerous, and potentially involves the loss of millions of dollars of medicines, what he means is: There are people dying. We've got a checkbook. I have a plane. I have medicines. I am not going to wait around for some Ph.D. to do a needs analysis and measure everything. Too many people are going to die in the meantime. Just make it happen."

In Bob's mind, AmeriCares was conceived as a strike force that could offer immediate relief to the victims of natural and man-made disasters. "Other people have to have committees and meetings and go through a long process; we can make a decision in sixty seconds and just go," he says.

As a result, AmeriCares is almost routinely the first private group to arrive at the scene of a disaster. They were the first relief agency into Poland while that country was under martial law; the first into Beirut after the Israeli invasion in 1982; the first into India after Bhopal, arriving after a request from Mother Teresa within twelve hours of that disaster; the first into Poland after Chernobyl in 1986; the first into Armenia after the earthquake in 1988; the first into Kuwait City, arriving just hours after the city's liberation in 1990; the first into Rwanda where a million people were slaughtered in 1994; the first to Chechnya in 1995; the first into North Korea when one-fifth of the country's population faced starvation in 1997; the first into Bosnia and on down the list of nightmares that have filled the headlines during the last two decades.

On the domestic front, AmeriCares operates three free clinics, which have provided more than $1.5 million in medical services to Connecticut's uninsured, a state-wide home repair project called HomeFront, and Camp AmeriKids, a summer camping experience for children living with life-threatening illness. In 2002, on its 20th anniversary, AmeriCares had risen to 20th in the world in size and effectiveness.

"In a way it is a kind of instant, energetic, almost preemptive impact that AmeriCares represents," Zbigniew Brzezinski, the foundation's Honorary Chairman, notes. "We are not a huge organization. We are not going to make a difference in the life and death of a whole society. But we may make a difference for the survival of a significant number of people at a very critical time."

"Where did all this come from?" I ask Bob.

"I believe if you work hard enough and pray hard enough, nothing is impossible," he said. "We beg and we beg hard. The first year our goal was $50,000. We got three million. The next year it was twelve million. Then it went to twenty-one. The fourth year it took a big jump to fifty-five million. Now we are over five billion.

"It multiplies because people get a sense of confidence when they see what you are doing and realize you are not getting anything out of it for yourself. People like to help people who are doing something for someone else. The only time you really give is when you get nothing in return. If you ask for yourself, it brings out the selfishness in others. When you ask for someone else, you are saying, 'Join me and I will share with you the joy of saving a life.'"

"Who gets the most out of it?"

"I think I do."

"What do you get?"

"Peace with God."

"Fulfillment?"

"Yeah, spiritual fulfillment, more than anything else, which is the really most important type there is. Rousseau said the man who dies with money in the bank has lived a poor life. We shouldn't delude ourselves into thinking that we went out and earned it. A little of that is true, but the basic thrust of what he said is that it comes from a power greater than ourselves that put us in the right place at the right time. Maybe we had a little to do with it, but that's all. If you squirrel away all the things that come to you and don't use them to help other people, you are really a loser at life."

We are watching CNN as we talk. The broadcast bounces from Iraq to Afghanistan. There have been terrorist bombings in both places. Remembering AmeriCares' early involvement in Afghanistan when its rebels were at war with Russia, I ask: "Does it bother you that some of the people you have helped are not our friends or that some of the people who were our friends have gone the other way?"

"In this world, today's friend is tomorrow's enemy and today's enemy is tomorrow's friend," he said. "But, if you look at the purity of what you are doing, it doesn't matter. They are all human beings. God created them. They have a right to live. You are not dealing with a Russian or a Pole, an Afghan or an Iraqi. We are all children of God. No matter what color they are, what political intuitions they may have, they are still creatures of God."

"The Starfish Story became AmeriCares' motto because it says so much of what I believe," Bob says. "We can't solve all the problems in the world. Nobody can. Only God can do that. But the fact that we can't solve all the problems does not absolve us of the responsibility of solving the ones we can. Like the boy in the story we can all make a difference."

The Starfish Story

As the old man walked the beach at dawn, he noticed a young man ahead of him picking up starfish and flinging them into the sea. Finally, catching up with the youth, he asked him why he was doing this. The answer was that the stranded starfish would die if left in the morning sun.

"But the beach goes on for miles and there are millions of starfish," countered the old man. "How can your efforts make any difference?"

The young man looked at the starfish in his hand and then gently returned it to safety in the waves. "It makes a difference to this one," he said.

Nothing on This Earth Can Separate One Heart from Another

"This lovely poem was a favorite of our son, Marek," Andrze Skabon wrote Bob in December of 1982.

> This we already know
> For it is always the same,
> With the frost and the snow
> Come the Holidays.
> Already the tables are groaning,
> Animals speak to us with human voices
> Saying, nothing on this earth
> Can separate one heart from another
> For the Holidays are coming.

When he had come to Bob's attention two years before, Marek had what was thought to be an inoperable brain tumor. For five years the doctors in his native Poland had done what they could for the boy with their limited resources. Finally, they decided there was nothing more they could do and gave up.

In desperation, the family looked for help and turned to the church. There they heard about a man in America who had started an organization called AmeriCares that was sending badly needed medicine and medical supplies to the country—then still under martial law.

With faint hope, Marek's father sent a letter to Robert C. Macauley, founder of AmeriCares, pleading for whatever help he could provide. To Andrze's surprise, the man in America, a man he had never met or spoken with, arranged to have his son flown to London for the sophisticated surgery he needed.

Bob found a surgeon who had had success in similar cases and pressed him for assistance. Four operations and several months later, the happy and healthy child returned home to his family.

But tragedy sometimes compounds tragedy. A few

months after his return, the boy had a bicycle accident severe enough to land him back in the hospital.

"We were saddened to learn that you had taken a fall from your bicycle," Bob wrote Marek in August of 1982 when he heard the news. "But I hope and pray that all is going well for you now."

The letter continued in this extraordinary way: "Marek, whether you know it or not you have been unofficially adopted by my family and by me. How seldom it is that anyone is afforded the opportunity of trying to help a fine young man such as you. For that privilege we will be eternally grateful. I just wanted you to know that you have our love and are in our prayers every evening."

Sadly, three months later, Marek died.

"During Marek's illness he was exceptionally good and cheerful," his father wrote. "We had to thrust our care upon him, as he never asked for anything. . . . Although he lived barely eleven years, he performed on this earth an important task—he made us aware that the long road of life had but one ending, that in life we must remember to give all of ourselves to Him so that we may ultimately be joined with Him. That is why we do not despair. We will always remember you, sir, who demonstrated so much heart, so much goodness and help for our little boy. We will always ask for God's blessing and care for you and your family."

By the time Macauley received Andrze's letter, the holidays had arrived. He found himself thinking about the boy and his father. "The holidays are coming..." Marek's poem read.

If I were a Polish father, Bob wondered, suffering under political repression and martial law, with no money and little food, living in a country where everything is rationed—what little token of love could I give my child? He saw a box of chocolates someone had sent him and had an inspiration. There was no chocolate in Poland.

The next morning Macauley called the president of Hershey's Chocolate and told his story.

"I told him what I was trying to do and asked him if he could help me out a little," he recalls.

The man from Hershey said, "I will give you a million Kisses."

From there he went to the Mars candy company. At first Mars did not respond as well, but then Bob mentioned Hershey's had already committed their participation in a big way.

"How much?" Mars asked.

Bob said, "A million," without saying a million what.

"We will match that," Mars said.

Macauley followed up with Nestlé and Peter Paul Cadbury. By the following Monday, three days after his inspiration, 165,000 pounds of chocolate were on the way to Poland.

Each container carried the label "From the children of America to the children of Poland, with love." In Marek's honor the shipments continued every Christmas for three more years.

Two years later Annie receives a call from the White House. The caller informs Annie that President Reagan wants to give Bob the President's Volunteer Action Award.

Bob says he will not accept unless the award is given to AmeriCares.

When Annie calls back with Bob's response, the White House aide making the arrangements bristles. No one has ever had the temerity to dictate to the President how an award should be given.

Macauley holds his ground.

"I have an obsession with ego," Bob explains. "I have seen it ruin so many things. No one takes credit around here. Everything is a team effort. If you've got the deed, you don't need the credit. If you've got the actions, you don't need the ego. It's the people who don't have the action who want the credit. I don't want my name on anything—no building, no roads, nothing."

As usual, Bob prevails. In presenting the award to Ameri-Cares, President Reagan takes particular delight in telling the story of chocolate for Poland. "Next time you go to Poland," he notes wryly, "you may want to take a dentist along."

"Inertia is far more dangerous than change."

ROBERT C. MACAULEY

Love Expressed

*I*t is June of 2003. We are about halfway through the process. I still have some research to do, but I have interviewed everyone I need to interview.

Once more we are in Bob's living room in New York. After Angie and Leila have retired to another part of the house, I give him a report on my progress. Among other things, I tell him I am developing a list of "Bobisms"—things people say he is known for saying.

Bob is intrigued. "What have you got so far?"

"Well, Mike Gasser said you pulled him aside early on when he first joined Greif Brothers and told him one of the things you have always tried to live by is to 'be big in small things.' He said you have always been big in things that might seem small to some but were huge to other people. He said when he took over the company he has made a point to try to follow your example."

Bob smiled but said nothing so I continued.

"Annie says you are a connoisseur of opportunity and thrive on chaos, even to the extent of creating chaos were none exists. Her favorite memory is a memo you sent around to the staff early on. She said all it had on it were the letters MTH."

"I wanted to see if people could figure it out."

"Make things happen."

"That's right. I have always believed that. I think the opportunities we have in this world are virtually unlimited. You just have to go for it."

I told him he reminded me of one of my favorite quotations. Goethe said, "The moment one definitely commits oneself, then Providence moves too. All sorts of things occur to help one that would never otherwise have occurred. . . . Boldness has genius, power, and magic in it."

I ask Bob if that is what he believes.

"Absolutely. You have to have the audacity to make a commitment and go. That's when the miracles happen. You have got to swim upstream. If you go down with the tide you will be right back where you started. That's the only way to get ahead. That's the only way to do anything."

"Where is the line in this between God's will and man's action?"

"There is no easy answer to that. But you have to be willing to step out on the precipice to make the miracle possible. You are the instrument. You have got to be willing to step out on faith or it will never happen. If you do the right thing and pray hard enough, it will generally work out."

"A lot of people have a hard time believing in miracles. What do you say to them?"

Bob waved his hand impatiently. "Your whole life is a walking testimony to miracles," he said. "Every day. I always find it strange that people who experience miracles will not acknowledge them as miracles. That's kind of crazy. Why not give credit to someone other than yourself. They say *I* did this, you know, the big I. If we just got away from the I, I, I,

141

and thought about other people, the world would be a lot better place."

"The first time we met you talked a lot about faith and commitment."

"I remember. I was sitting on the couch in my office. I told you that whenever you start out to do anything you will find nine different people jumping up and giving you nine different reasons why it won't work. You just have to believe in what you are doing and mow them all down."

"And I said you reminded me of Hannibal's line on crossing the Alps: 'We will either find a way or make one.'"

Bob laughed. "A few years ago, I was visiting with the Negropontes when John was ambassador to Honduras," he said. "The kids weren't up yet and I was talking to Diane over breakfast. I don't know why she thought of it, but all of a sudden she said, 'I know what they are going to put on your tombstone: Never give in.'

"That pretty much sums it up. The outcome is not in our hands. All we can do is give it our best shot."

Bobisms

- Don't bunt
- Go for it
- Red tape kills
- Make things happen
- If you have an ego, park it on the street
- Take everything seriously but yourself
- Be big in small things
- Anything worth doing is worth doing to excess
- You can get anyone to do anything for you as long they get the credit

- Money in the bank and medicines in the warehouse do not save lives
- Avoid the four Bs—big buildings and bloated bureaucracies
- Love is the only thing that can save the world
- Never give in

Snapshots

*I*n 1984, when other relief groups are rushing to stave off the famine in Ethiopia, AmeriCares uncharacteristically holds back. Bob distrusts the Ethiopian government and is concerned they will control distribution. His suspicions proved to be well-founded. The relief effort organized by his colleagues turns into a disaster nearly as large as the disaster they are trying to address. Much of the donated supplies are stolen or left to rot on the docks.

The worst of the famine is in the rebel provinces of Tigre and Eritrea, which the Ethiopian government is deliberately starving. Bob's answer is a flanking maneuver. He contacts the President of Sudan and gets permission to move food, medicines, and medical personnel over the mountains into the rebel provinces. Soon, two 747s filled with half a million pounds of supplies land in Sudan. They are loaded into trucks and transported over the mountains into Ethiopia, the trucks traveling at night without headlights to avoid strafing. As a result, all of AmeriCares' supplies reach the people who need help the most.

In 1989 the famine in Sudan is compounded by civil war between government forces controlled by President Mengistu and the rebels under Colonel John Garang. Millions of people have been killed. Millions have been displaced. Millions more are said to be in jeopardy.

Again, Bob is determined to get medicines in and provide some relief. He has called Mother Teresa, said to be the only person Mengistu will listen to, and tried to evoke her assistance. He has called the White House and the United Nations. He has asked for a Papal blessing on his efforts to establish corridors of tranquility so that life-saving medicine can be brought to the civilians caught in harm's way.

In the midst of all this, Bob receives a call from Egil Hagen. Egil had served as a Commander of the U.N. peacekeeping forces in Lebanon and other trouble spots before joining the Norwegian Aid Society in Nairobi. Egil said there was a barge on a river near a town called Ler. The barge had been built in Norway and was used for relief by the U.N. until it was captured.

"Egil said 'I think we can get it out,'" Bob recalls. "He wanted to shanghai it. We talked it through. I said go for it. He got it without a shot. We flew supplies into Nairobi. A private pilot would fly them from there to a place where they could be loaded on the barge and taken to Ler. It only went about four miles an hour and had to travel at night because the Air Force was bombing anything that moved on the river. But we shipped millions of pounds of food and medicine that way and kept the village alive for months."

Make Things Happen

When Chernobyl blew up in 1986, toxic clouds started drifting west over Poland, dropping poisonous rain that contaminates the grass, and indirectly the milk that comes from the cows that eat it. Almost immediately, a church official in Poland starts telexing AmeriCares asking for help. They need milk for their infants, baby food, and vitamins to counter the effects of the radiation.

Various governments and international relief organizations consider their options and move with their customary deliberate pace. The Red Cross in Switzerland takes the lead and invites AmeriCares to participate in a committee they have set up to consider the matter.

Bob assembles his team, divides up the cleric's list, and begins making phone calls. Within hours the team locates a convoy of trucks carrying powdered milk en route to Mexico. Somehow Bob makes a deal to acquire the cargo and redirect it to New York. Less than seventy-two hours after the telex arrived, one million pounds of powdered milk, to be mixed with water sixteen to one before use, arrives in Poland.

Later that year, a devastating earthquake strikes El Salvador. Overwhelmed by the tragedy, the government shuts down the country's main airport for eight days while they figure out what to do. Meanwhile, people are suffering and dying.

"It was a bureaucratic screw up," Bob recalls, the kind of thing that drives him crazy.

Bob's answer is to call a friend in El Salvador who used to be in their air force.

"You are a pilot," Bob says. "You know what to do. I'll call you when the plane is about to land. You go up to the tower and talk him down."

AmeriCares makes six trips in three days, unloading half a million pounds of supplies and completing delivery of their medicines while others are still waiting permission to begin.

"There was no problem at all," Bob says. "We were the only ones in the air."

In 1994 the New York Times *reports daycare workers employed by the city have not been paid in months. Many are selling their personal belongings in order to keep a roof over their heads while continuing to care for the children in their charge.*

The first Annie hears of it is when she arrives at the office. The phone is ringing when she arrives. She knows it has to be Bob.

"I want you to do three things," Bob says. "When the bank opens, pull $50,000 out of my personal account. Get it in cash and put it in an armored truck. Get a couple of the guys to take it down there and divide it among these people so they can get by. Get the money. Get the truck. And go."

Understandably, the publicity from Macauley's gift embarrasses the city into action. Suddenly, they find money to honor their contract with their employees and resume payments.

Be Big in Small Things

*T*welve years after Egil "liberated" the barge in the Sudan, AmeriCares is trying to find a way to get medicine into Sarejevo. "We tried to find someone to fly in, but no one would go," Bob says. "I had Jim Schaeffer call everyone. All the commercial carriers. Finally he came back and said he had one possibility—the Norwegian Air Force. They at least had not said 'no' outright."

"I had Jim get the Vice Commander of the Norwegian Air Force on the line," Bob says. "I could tell he was skeptical. Looking for a way to connect, I asked if he knew Egil Hagen."

"Everyone in Europe knew Egil," he said.

"So I asked, 'Did you go to his funeral?'"

"Yes, I escorted the King of Norway."

"Did you like the eulogy?"

"Why do you ask?"

"I wrote it," Bob said.

Nothing more needed to be said. "What do you want?" the Vice Commander asked.

Bob told him he needed three C130s. After that, the Norwegian Air Force and AmeriCares teamed up to fly many missions into Sarajevo together. The Norwegians never charged a dime.

It is New Year's Eve in Sarajevo. AmeriCares has flown 126 relief missions to what was formerly Yugoslavia during the long years of war, but never anything like this.

To mark the new year and the dawn of hope, Bob has decided to try to find previous members of the city's orchestra and organize a free concert for Sarajevo. The whole city has been bombed out and many of the members of the orchestra are "in the trees," but you can almost see them coming out of the hills with their instruments when Hans Richter from the Viennese Philharmonic agrees to partici-

pate. To elevate the event, AmeriCares flies in a grand piano and a guest artist, the internationally known pianist, Jon Parker Kimura, for the occasion.

Though it is cold in what is left of the bombed-out concert hall in the heart of the city, every seat is filled. For the first time in years, the guns are silent and the sounds of hope—Beethoven's Third and Fifth Symphony—fill the air. The concert is carried live all over Europe—a huge success.

Love Never Fails

When you are a boy playing soccer, probably the last thing you are thinking about is being safe. For twelve-year-old Sead Bekric it was not safe; artillery shells blew up the ground beneath his feet in Bosnia. The last memory he has before the darkness closes his eyes is watching a friend's head being blown off. He has no memory of the shrapnel that struck his eyes or the helicopter that came to fly him to Tuzla.

All he remembers is the pain. He screams in agony, seemingly forever, until he hears his younger brother's voice. Summing up his courage, he says, "I'm all right. Don't be afraid."

A CNN crew passing by catches this touching exchange. Within hours the image of this brave blind boy is broadcast around the world. Millions of people see the story. Many undoubtedly wish they could do something to help.

One does.

Turning to Terry Tarnowski who is watching the broadcast with him, Bob says, "Let's go get him."

"Most of us can be terribly moved by something and even say to ourselves, 'Oh, I wish I could do something,' but Bob never stops there," Terry says. "With Bob that is just the bare beginning. The desire is just the first step and for him it is never a big step. It is one and the same thing. If you want to respond, then you respond. What can I do? And then follow through. There is no question about can I do it or I'm not sure if I can or what's the way to do it. I want to respond. I will respond. What is the best way to respond is the next step."

Tuzla airport is not open for humanitarian relief flights, but somehow the U.N. is persuaded to let AmeriCares land long enough to collect the boy and bring him out. Less than twenty-four hours after the boy loses his sight, a rescue team is en route.

The trip is harrowing. Going in, the helicopter has to refuel at Split before the final leg to Tuzla. Fighting is so fierce around the airport that the helicopter touches down, gasses up, and takes off in less than five minutes.

Two hours later, they are in Tuzla and Sead and his family are brought on board. Sead lost his sight on Monday. By Friday of the same week, he is in California being treated by the Jules Stein Eye Institute.

"It seems your approach is to make a total commitment," I tell Bob when I hear this story. "You decide you are going to get this kid one way or another and just go."

"That's right," Bob responds. "If you were doing something where you stood to gain something from it, it would never have happened. In Saed's case, we had two guys with him. When we got him to the Netherlands the people at KLM had all seen his picture and wanted to help. They put him on a plane and flew him to L.A. free of charge. They all seem to come together like that. If you can explain to people what you are trying to do, they all want to help. People love to get aboard. Maybe they didn't start it, but they get a lot of satisfaction out of being part of it.

"You see an opportunity and you take a big gamble and boom, just go for it," Bob says. "If you are doing it for someone else, that's almost a guarantee of success. If you are doing it for yourself, that's almost always a guarantee of failure. If you don't go for it when the window is open, it never opens again—not that window.

"It may be a bit impulsive in a way, but when you see an opportunity, just go. Don't ever look back. Don't think of all the reasons why it won't work or it might be a failure. Just make your mind up you are going to go and go. Pray a lot. Have faith. Get it done, and go on to the next one. Always be first. If you lead, others will follow."

"Where does that come from?" I ask.

"I guess it is all part of my sense of urgency. It starts with knowing what's the right thing to do. If you know what the right thing to do is, do it. Don't weigh it back and forth, up and down, and consider it and go half way. Jump in all the way up to your neck and plow through. That's when miracles happen."

Anything Worth Doing
Is Worth Doing to Excess

I met Virginia Kamsky on an AmeriCares flight to Guatemala. Bob met her when she joined the W. R. Grace Board of Directors in 1990, four years before.

"I walked into the boardroom and they were all male, most in their 60s and 70s. For some reason, I sat down next to Bob," Ginny says. "I quickly found he was like no one else you are ever going to meet. He was magnetic, magnanimous, bigger than life but in a selfless way. There are people you meet who are bigger than life that have huge egos. He was the opposite. He doesn't really care what other people think.

Peter Grace used to intimidate a lot of people. I don't think anyone has ever intimidated Bob.

"I was always flying in for board meetings from China or wherever, and Bob started getting on me, telling me there are more things in life than making money and doing business. He would tell me it's really important to give back, how it is important to help other people, and tell me that I had to learn to stop and smell the flowers.

"At that time, I would be in three countries in one day. Believe it or not, he would call my secretary and find out where I was and where I was going to be. When I arrived in my hotel—wherever I was—there would be a note with a huge bouquet saying, 'Stop long enough to smell the flowers, Bob Macauley.'

"Then he began getting after me to have a child, telling me the next business deal is not what matters. I can't tell you how hard he worked on me to have a child. Ultimately, I got pregnant and had a very difficult pregnancy.

"Both my son and I had a twenty percent chance of survival. Every day the pregnancy went on, my chance of survival decreased and my son's increased.

Everybody, including my own doctors came to me and said, 'This is a situation where late stage abortion is legal and it is much too dangerous for your health.'

"I wouldn't go through with it, so I had to stop traveling and stay within five minutes of a hospital. On September 2, I was rushed to the hospital. When I was admitted the doctors said I wasn't going to live and if my son lived he would be blind and deaf and have cerebral palsy.

"Somehow spontaneously, I stopped hemorrhaging. I didn't want anyone to know where I was or what was going on because I knew my family couldn't handle it, so I didn't tell them. But Bob could tell there was something wrong. He kept pushing me. He did his own intelligence and found out where I was. My staff didn't know where I was. My family didn't know where I was. Bob was the only one. He called me at least three times a day. On a daily basis he would send me a CD of classical music. I got a FedEx package every day and every week I would get a bouquet of flowers from Victoria Gardens. Every bouquet had the number of stems for the number of weeks I had completed, so at the end of week twenty-four I got twenty-four tulips; at the end of week twenty-five I got twenty-five peonies.

"When I made it to week thirty-five, at Christmas time, a man came in with a double-decker cart of poinsettia plants. The week my son was born, he had a Christmas tree delivered to the hospital, decorated with thirty-six handmade gold angels, each one playing a different instrument, and a great big angel on top. I was in the hospital for twelve weeks. I hemorrhaged three times and went into intensive care. Bob never gave up. He gave us so much love and support it made all the difference in the world. Bob was the only one who thought I was going to pull through all this.

"When you are facing a terminal illness, most people can't cope with it and disappear from your life. Bob did the opposite. He just got bigger and bigger in my life. He wouldn't let up. Sometimes I was on the phone all day long with him. I was restricted as to whom I could talk with. But Bob was unlimited. Whenever Bob called my blood pressure went down. He never thought of it as a burden. Rather, he said it was a favor to him that I would allow him to help me."

Never Give In

In 1988, an earthquake in Armenia kills 55,000 people and leaves 500,000 homeless. Within five hours, AmeriCares has organized its relief effort. The first planeload of medicine is put in the air before the plane has a landing permit, despite the fact that no aid has gone to the Soviet Union ever before. Without a landing permit, the plane will be violating Soviet airspace. The airline is concerned enough about this risk that it demands that AmeriCares indemnify them against loss in case the plane is shot down.

For Bob, as usual, there is no choice. The longer he waits, the more people will die. He knows Mikhail

Gorbachev is in Washington at the time and gambles he will be able to get permission before it is too late.

The pilot radios from Canada asking whether the permit has come through.

"No, not yet."

From Ireland.

"No, not a word."

Finally, from Belgrade.

"Still nothing."

Despite his obvious reservations, Macauley persuades the pilot to begin the final leg of the journey anyway, and he heads for Armenia.

The permit finally comes through when the plane is just 200 miles from the Soviet border. The medicine reaches those who so desperately need it soon thereafter, making AmeriCares the first private relief group ever allowed into the Soviet Union.

"He who desires to see the living God face to face,
should not seek him in the empty firmament
of his mind, but in human love."

GEORGE BERNARD SHAW

Love Endures

In December of 1986, Bob is hospitalized. When he came home from the Sudan the year before, he brought intestinal parasites with him. He then aggravated his condition by going to Honduras. By the time he returned, he also had malaria, pneumonia, and an intestinal block. He needed surgery in a hurry.

Reluctantly, he enters the hospital, his least favorite place to be, but not before he has two phone lines installed in his room. The day after the doctors remove eighteen inches of his colon, he picks up the phone and begins begging.

He is soon getting calls from all over the world. Concerned he isn't getting enough rest, his doctor removes one line. His doctor removes the other line when he is told he

*can't see Bob because there are five international calls wait-
ing. Even so, the calls continue to come in, only now they
have to be processed through the nurses' station, aggravat-
ing the staff no end.*

*On December 11, Bob's birthday, he keeps them partic-
ularly busy. Finally, one of his frustrated nurses charges
into the room and says, "Now there is some old bag on the
phone who claims to be Mother Teresa."*

*It is in fact Mother calling to wish Bob a happy birth-
day. "Jesus is showing his great love for you in your suffering," she says.*

*"Do you think He might love me just a little less?" Bob
asks, tongue in cheek.*

Mother Teresa is not amused.

In the fall of 2003, I find myself suddenly seriously
ill. I am one of those fortunate ones who has never
had reason to question my health. To this point, I
have never been hospitalized for any reason. I have
never broken a bone or had any illness more serious
than the common cold.

Over the course of the next four months, I find myself hospitalized four times. In between, I visit the emergency room twice, see my doctor weekly, and donate enough blood to keep the Red Cross afloat for a month.

I am wracked with fever and find it difficult to move my arms and legs. The second hospital visit reveals I have pneumonia. The third finds a blood clot in my lungs. The consensus seems to be that both are symptomatic of some more fundamental problem. My liver and white blood cell counts are off the charts. Something serious is going on, but no one seems to know what.

The medical establishment responds by hauling out their heavy artillery and bombing the unknown invader with heavy doses of antibiotics while they search for the root cause. When the antibiotics prove useless, steroids are administered to ease my discomfort while the doctors continue their investigation. I am tested and retested for every possible infectious disease or systemic illness from cancer to hepatitis and AIDS. I have X-rays, sonograms, CAT scans, NMRIs, and two biopsies—to no avail.

Through it all, Bob and Leila are there. The sicker I am, the more present they are in our lives, much as they were in Ginny's years before. "I hope we are not calling you too much," Leila says at one point, "but Bob worries if he doesn't know what's going on."

It is Bob who decides in December that "this thing has gone on long enough" and makes arrangements for me to visit the Mayo Clinic. It's Leila who bakes chocolate chip cookies for me and sends them up by FedEx so that I will have a touch of home away from home.

The most difficult part of this dark period is the sense of being forced into myself. Illness forces the eye to turn inward. I have never felt more self-centered, self-concerned, and self-involved. As the illness lingers, it becomes increasingly difficult to bear. I tire of worrying and talking about my health and hunger for something more productive to do.

While I struggle with it, I think of Bob. I think of the irony in the fact that the project I began because of my concern for his failing health might not be completed because of my own, and my awareness of what it means to be ill gives me a better understanding of the burden he carries. While I have always been healthy, Bob has never been completely well. When I first began my visits to New Canaan, his ankles would swell to twice their normal size every time we went out or when he stood too long.

He partied hard in his youth, drank heavily for twenty years, and smoked most of his life. He put a lot of mileage on his body and burned the candle at both ends, sometimes working all day at the office and playing piano most of the night. Even in the best of times, he never got much rest.

He has had operations for a blockage in his colon, a heart aneurysm, and cancer of the eye. He has had liver problems, chronic obstructive lung disease, and degenerative arthritis.

I realize the difficulty I have had standing for a few weeks, Bob has experienced for years. His peripheral neuropathy and arthritis make it difficult for him to walk more than a few feet without assistance. He endures great pain daily and suffers from recurring bouts of depression. Yet the first question he asks is always, "How are you doing?" Bob seems to have little interest in his own problems. He prefers to focus on the problems of others.

In 2000, Sheila and her husband, the photographer David Douglas Duncan, are visiting Bob and Leila. Sheila and David live in France where they got to know Picasso while David photographed him at work. They were in New York for a book promotion and took Leila out to lunch, leaving Bob alone.

"We came back," David recalls, "and found him outside by the pool. He had fallen face forward and was lying like a giant turtle, unable to right himself and get up. We didn't know where he was at first. There were no calls or complaints. He was just waiting there patiently for someone to come and help him. There was not one word of complaint. Not one word."

There is no self-pity in the man. As Bob has made abundantly clear, he feels blessed. Now, he is convinced he is dying. "We all are," Leila responds, but he is much more at peace with this process than the rest of us are.

Still, you get the feeling this must be the most difficult thing he could do—endure. It is easier to die in one clap of thunder than to go by inches. For a man of action, for a man used to making things happen, waiting is hard.

"Since I can't walk anymore, I sit in this chair sixteen to eighteen hours a day," Bob says. "You are forced to evaluate your life in almost microscopic detail. I can remember seventy years ago, the girlfriends and the license plates on their cars and their telephone numbers, but I can't remember what movie we watched last night."

"When you look back," I ask, "which do you regret more—the things you did or the things you didn't do?"

"By far the things I regret are the things I could have done and didn't. There was a nonprofit group in Washington six or seven years ago that said we had saved three million lives. That's pretty heavy stuff when you say your prayers at night. I don't know what the number is now, but I would guess that it is more, based on AmeriCares' growth. Whatever it is, it is still pretty heavy stuff. But still I say to myself we should have done more. If we have saved three million lives, why didn't we save five million lives? Maybe if I started earlier, worked a little harder, and begged a little harder, we could have saved more."

Snapshots

*P*aul Kindschi is pastor of Lost Tree Chapel in North Palm Beach, Florida. In the early '90s, he remembers one of the secretaries came into his office and said rather excitedly, "Pastor, there is a bum in the chapel. I don't know how he got onto the grounds even. But he is here in the chapel."

Kindschi went into the vestibule and looked through the swinging door. He saw a man there in meditation and prayer. He had two or three sweatshirts on and a three- or four-day's growth of beard. Outside, Kindschi could see a rusty bicycle he must have been riding.

Kindschi did not disturb the man's prayer but waited

outside until he finished. When he came out he said, "Can I help you?"

"I'm Bob Macauley," the man responded. "I like to stop in to take prayer occasionally."

"That's very much the nature of the man," Kindschi told me. "He is who he is. He hates ostentation. His faith is very meaningful to him, but he doesn't say much about it to others."

In Areopagitica, *John Milton wrote, "It was from out the rind of one apple tasted, that knowledge of good and evil, as two twins cleaving together, leaped forth into the world. And perhaps this is that doom which Adam fell into of knowing good and evil, that is to say of knowing good by evil. . . . He that can apprehend and consider vice with all her baits and seeming pleasures, and yet abstain, and yet distinguish, and yet prefer that which is truly better, he is the true wayfaring Christian. I cannot praise a fugitive and cloistered virtue, unexercised and 'unbreathed,' that never sallies out and sees her adversary, but slinks out of the race . . . that which purifies us is trial, and trial is by what is contrary."*

"A 'wayfaring Christian'—that is the phrase that leaps to mind when I think about Bob," Callahan said. "The knowledge of good and evil is both a burden and a blessing. Only by bearing witness to Evil can we truly know what is Good.

"Bob has made a conscious choice in his life to direct his considerable energies and bend even his less godly impulses into a godly manner. He is a street fighter. He doesn't mind cajoling, manipulating, begging to get something done. He has made a conscious effort to surround himself with and reach out to godly people, to seek them out, to seek ways to be used, and to use his considerable energies in a way that helps make things better for others."

"Strange was the way I came, and long and far,

O End of all my world, all beauty's verge!

My harbor, haven, terminal you are.

For me no lights beyond your light emerge.

I see no star above life's lonely hill.

I see no other, and I never will.

ARCHIBALD RUTLEDGE

His Name Is Today

t is the fall of 2003—almost a year after we began—and we are talking about endings. There is none of the intensity of our previous meetings. We talk about next steps—the writing process, agents and publishers. Everything has been said. There is no new ground to cover, but both of us are reluctant to see the beginning of the ending.

"One of the things I would like to talk through is how this thing should end," I say.

"I have thought about that a lot since we talked about it on the phone," Bob responds. "I really don't have the answer other than to say I have a very grateful heart."

"The traditional way to end a book like this," I suggest, "is to provide a summary or a parting thought —this is what I have learned. Another way is to challenge the reader—this is what I have done, but the work goes on and on. The ending is there is no ending."

"It would be sad in a way if there was," Bob says. "The end is not in our hands. I take it day by day."

Bob thinks for a moment and continues, "I was with Mother Teresa when she received the Nobel Peace Prize," Bob said. "As she was leaving some wiseguy reporter stuck a microphone in her face and said, 'Mother Teresa what is your fondest wish'—like he expected her to say, 'Now, I'm going to Disneyland' or something equally silly. You know what she said? Without a moment's hesitation, she answered, 'To be unemployed.'

"It is a wonderful answer—something we all pray for—but we will never be unemployed. I wish there could be an end to suffering and need, but that is not going to happen. There will always be poverty and violence and hate. We will never 'solve' the problem.

"Man is a finite beast trying to answer infinite

questions. He'll never get it. I have no delusions of grandeur. I know we can't save the whole world. But the fact that you can't do everything does not excuse you from doing what you can.

"Whatever you do, do the best you can. At least when you check out you can say, 'I had a good run. I did what I could with what I had.' The outcome is not in our hands. All we can do is give it our best shot."

"Some people may say, 'That's fine for today, but what about tomorrow?'"

"You can't worry about tomorrow. You have got to take each day as it comes along and do the best you can. The Chilean poet Gabriela Mistral said it best. There is that beautiful line from her poem where she talks about children and how their bones are being formed as we speak and how their needs cannot wait. 'To him we cannot answer, "Tomorrow," she wrote. His name is 'Today.'

"The last time you were here, you asked me about regrets. I keep thinking about that. I can reconstitute my life back to when I was six years old. The more I thought about it, the more I feel it is about ten to one things I could have done. You ask yourself, could I have done this? Why didn't I do it? God gave me some talent. Did I utilize it to the fullest? Could we have saved more? That's what keeps me awake at night.

"When you get down to it, I think there is a spirit in every person that wants to do good. Most just don't carry it out. I'm glad I did. That's really the test. When you come down to it, the only thing that's going to save the world is love—pure and simple—just love."

Epilogue:
Looking for Starfish

*I*t is hard to calculate the impact Bob and Ameri-Cares have had. The numbers are too imposing. It's impossible to comprehend millions of lives and billions of dollars. It's hard to wrap your mind around numbers of that size. Instead, I decide to go looking for starfish.

Like the boy on the beach, I know I cannot find them all. But maybe I can find enough. If I can find a few and measure the impact Bob has had on their lives maybe it will be easier to comprehend the contribution he has made to the world.

In particular, I want to find some of the children who were on the C5A that crashed in Vietnam. They would be grown now. I zero in on the Carnie kids, Lorrie and Landon, because I am intrigued by their story and wonder what happened to them. Do they know about Bob and what he did? What has become of them and what are they doing?

For those who do not believe in miracles the story of the Carnie kids is difficult to explain. Dubbed "Hansel and Gretel" by a German nurse who cared for the twins as infants in the orphanage, they were loaded onto different parts of the plane in the rush of departure. When the plane went down, neither could be found. The initial report was that both had perished. "Hansel and Gretel not found," read the telegram sent to George Carnie, the man who had adopted them, shortly after the crash.

But somehow the infants had not only survived, they had found each other. Rescuers stumbled on them clinging together in a rice paddy more than a hundred yards from the crash site. "Hansel and Gretel found," came the miraculous news. Even more wondrous for George was the information they had been positively identified by the wristbands they wore as they were loaded on to the Pan Am jet Bob had chartered. A day before, they were lost. Now, some-how, he would hold them in his arms before the dawn of another day.

I find them by chance after calling every George Carnie I can identify. It is in September. I call a holistic healing center in the Northwest that has a man by that name listed as a founder. It is a reach because I know the twins' father was a teacher, not a businessman or a health practitioner. But I am determined to exhaust all possibilities.

Carnie is not in the office when I call. From the vagueness of the receptionist, it appears he hasn't been there for a while. She says she doesn't know where to find him but refers me to another number.

I call the second number dutifully but without much hope this call will be any more productive than any of the others. When you throw starfish back into the ocean, I reason, you shouldn't be surprised when they are hard to find.

A young woman answers the phone on the second ring, reciting the name of the company I had called. She listens patiently as I stumble through my story. I tell her I am looking for the George Carnie associated with Bob Macauley and the C5A and hoping to find out what became of the twins.

"That's me," she says simply and sends chills up my spine. I guess on some level I didn't expect to find her and am surprised when I do.

Lorrie says she is married now and has four children: three boys, ages six, five, four; and a two-year-old girl she adopted from Vietnam. She has graduated from Utah State University with a degree in merchandising. Her brother went back to Vietnam with her to pick up the girl and decided to stay. He is in Saigon teaching English at the university.

"We both believe our lives would have been very different if we had been left in Vietnam," Lorrie says. "Landon stayed because he wants to give something back. I want to start a foundation so that I can help other people the way other people have helped me."

Lorrie has never met Bob Macauley, but she has heard about him all of her life. She never knew until recently that he had mortgaged his house to get her out.

"He didn't even know my name or anything about me," she said. "My brother and I both feel it would be a great disservice to him and ourselves not to give something back."

On November 19, 2003, the *Today Show* airs a segment focusing on Bob and AmeriCares. As a surprise, Ann Curry, a fan of AmeriCares, has arranged for the Carnie twins to come and meet Bob, a man, she says in her introduction, who has changed lives all over the globe.

"I was worried about meeting you," Lorrie says. "I was worried about disappointing you."

"You could never do that," Bob replies.

"I have thought about it a lot since I was invited out to meet you," Lorrie says. "I look at my children and I have decided the best thing I can give back is healthy, productive, and caring adults."

"That's all the payment I could ever want," Bob says and gives her a hug.

So much for the miracles. Multiply them by tens of thousands if not millions. But what of the miracle-makers?

"Working with Bob was the turning point of my life," Jim Schaeffer says. "Even in his charity Bob is charitable. He had the contacts, resources, and money. He could have brought in the A-team from New York, seasoned professionals, but he chose to go the other way. He gave us all a life."

Terry Tarnowski agrees. "I was not the person you would think to hire and throw into the world like this. I had absolutely no idea what I was getting into. For me, it was a job. It was convenient to where I live. I thought, 'Well, why not?' but I didn't have a clue what I was getting into. After my first airlift, I was hooked."

"I would have been really happy just to be answering the phone and ordering supplies for this organization," Annie Yates told me. "It wasn't the job, it was what we were doing. I don't know why I was so fortunate to come here, to meet him, to have this wonderful experience. We all have a fire in the belly. We want to do something. Bob gave us an outlet and showed us how."

Perhaps the most telling story would be to end somewhere near where we began. Jim Schaefer was given the assignment to find a way to evacuate wounded Afghan rebels from Afghanistan during their war with Russia.

"I kept coming into Bob's office," Jim remembers, "saying this is just not happening. I am calling all the charter flights, but nobody will even talk to me. Bob kept sending me back with the words, 'Just do it. Find a way to make it happen.'"

Finally, Jim called the office of the head of international affairs at Pan Am. It was late. To his surprise, the man whose office he called answered the phone himself. Everyone else had gone home.

Jim launched into his routine, speaking quickly and trying to get it all in before the man could hang up on him. Jim said he was calling on behalf of Bob Macauley and AmeriCares and told him what they were trying to do in Afghanistan.

Rather than hang up, the man on the other end of the line said, "Is this the Bob Macauley who did that evacuation out of Vietnam?"

"Yes."

"Well, I'm the guy he conned on that deal," he said and Jim's heart sank. Then he added, "I'm in. I am going to do this airlift for you. I will do anything for that guy."

The fourth question I asked Bob the first time we met was if he had a favorite quotation. We had been talking for nearly two hours and covered all the essential elements of AmeriCares' development and operation. I thought this simple question might get to the heart of his personal philosophy.

"I have always found a passage from Albert Schweitzer particularly meaningful," Bob replied. "Schweitzer said 'It is not enough to say I am earning enough to live and support my family. I do my work well. I am a good father. I am a good husband. That's all very well but you must do something more. Seek always to do some good, somewhere. Every man has to seek in his own way to make his own self more noble and to realize his own true worth. You must give some time to your fellow man. Even if it is a little thing, do something for those who have need of help, something for which you get no pay, but the privilege of doing it. For remember, you don't live in a world all your own. Your brothers are here too.'

"Schweitzer's words so accurately capture the essence of what I believe," Bob said, "I incorporated the last line on

*the AmeriCares masthead: REMEMBER...YOUR BROTH-
ERS ARE HERE TOO. That's what it is all about. The only
thing that's going to save this world is not going to be political agreements—it's going to be love. Pure and simple. Just
love."*

About AmeriCares

meriCares is a nonprofit disaster relief and humanitarian aid organization providing immediate response to emergency medical needs, as well as supporting long-term humanitarian assistance programs for all people around the world, irrespective of race, creed or political persuasion. AmeriCares solicits donations of medicines, medical supplies and other relief materials from U.S. and international manufacturers, and delivers them quickly and efficiently to indigenous health care and welfare professionals around the world.

For over two decades, the success of AmeriCares has been characterized by timely response, meaningful impact, high integrity and intense passion for the work. To deliver medicine, relief supplies and health care to the needy, AmeriCares has developed a platform based on strategic partnerships, high-efficiency and tight auditing procedures.

Since its founding, AmeriCares has provided close to $5 billion of aid in more than 137 countries. To accomplish these results, AmeriCares assembles product donations from the private sector, determines the most urgent needs and solicits the funding to send the aid via airlift or ocean cargo to health and welfare professionals in the indigent locations.

On the ground, AmeriCares works with international and local non-governmental organizations (NGO's), hospitals, health networks and government ministries of long-standing effectiveness such as the Order of Malta, Mother Theresa's Sisters of Charity, Adventist Development and Relief Agency International, HOPE Worldwide, Project Mercy, Centres pour le Développement et la Santé and Help the Afghan Children.

Uncompromising security procedures assure that the assistance is distributed to the designated beneficiaries and not diverted—for example, all-inclusive tracking of medicine by lot number and thorough follow-ups.

The model is time-tested, cost-effective and experience-driven. In the recently completed fiscal year, auditing discloses that each $100 in cash contributions enabled AmeriCares to deliver more than $3,000 in emergency relief, including medicines, medical supplies, clothing, footwear, blankets and nutritional supplements.

AmeriCares responds to the needs of those suffering from adversity not just overseas, but in the U.S. as well. Key domestic programs include: Camp AmeriKids, AmeriCares Free Clinics, Inc. and AmeriCares HomeFront.

Camp AmeriKids was created to provide a traditional camping experience for children and adolescents living with HIV/AIDS. The camp is offered at no cost to the families and recruits campers from New York, New Jersey and Connecticut. The goals of the program are to develop independence, friendship and self-confidence through the building of new skills and increased abilities. Doctors and nurses are on staff twenty-four hours a day throughout the entire session.

AmeriCares Free Clinics, Inc. (AFC) opened its first clinic in November of 1994 to serve the medical needs of the working poor. Its mission is to provide free, quality health care to Connecticut's uninsured and underinsured population while protecting each patient's sense of dignity and self-respect. Currently, there are three clinics operating in Norwalk, Bridgeport and Danbury. AFC recruits volunteer physicians and registered nurses and draws on the resources of community hospitals, laboratories and pharmacies to ensure no-cost access to outpatient health care. Each clinic is designed to complement existing services and is tailored to meet specific needs identified in the community.

AmeriCares HomeFront is a community-based home repair program that provides quality of life repairs at no cost to homeowners in need. In the culmination of year-round planning and organization, more than 9,000 skilled and unskilled volunteers undertake these repair projects on the first Saturday of May each year.

How You Can Help

To make an on-line contribution to AmeriCares to provide immediate relief to emergency medical needs and support long-term humanitarian assistance to people around the world and here at home, log onto www.americares.org. If you prefer, contact Ameri-Cares at 1-800-486-HELP (4357), or send your donation to AmeriCares, 88 Hamilton Avenue, Stamford, CT 06902.

About the Author

Bill Halamandaris is a co-founder of The Heart of America Foundation® and four other national non-profit organizations. Previously, Halamandaris spent fifteen years serving as an investigator, chief investigator, counsel and director of oversight for the Senate and as a staff director of the House Select Committee on Aging, subcommittee on Health and Long-Term Care. He has authored five nonficton books and written and produced two documentaries for PBS.

Bill Halamandaris

Heart of America Foundation

Ph: (202)347-6278

Fax:(202)347-8599

bill@heartofamerica.org